WHO DO YOU SAY THAT I AM?

Who Do You Say That I Am?

Christology and the Church

Edited by

DONALD ARMSTRONG

WILLIAM B. EERDMANS PUBLISHING COMPANY
GRAND RAPIDS, MICHIGAN / CAMBRIDGE, U.K.

© 1999 Wm. B. Eerdmans Publishing Co.

255 Jefferson Ave. S.E., Grand Rapids, Michigan 49503 /

P.O. Box 163, Cambridge CB3 9PU U.K.

Paperback edition 1999

Printed in the United States of America

04 03 02 01 00 99   7 6 5 4 3 2

Library of Congress Cataloging-in-Publication Data

Who do you say that I am?: christology and the church /
edited by Donald Armstrong

p.   cm.

Proceedings of the 6th international conference of the Anglican Institute,
held in the fall of 1998 at the American Cathedral of the Holy Trinity, Paris, France.

Includes bibliographical references.

ISBN 0-8028-4746-3 (pbk.: alk. paper)

1. Jesus Christ — Person and offices Congresses.

2. Anglican Communion — Doctrines Congresses.

I. Armstrong, Donald, III. II. Anglican Institute.

BT205.W457 1999

232 — dc21   99-28296

CIP

Dedicated to
The Rev. Canon C. Frederick Barbee

A faithful warden
of the doctrine, discipline,
and worship of the
Episcopal Church

Contents

Preface

In the fall of 1998 the Anglican Institute held its sixth international conference at the American Cathedral of the Holy Trinity in Paris, France. The purpose of the conference was to offer a thoughtful, authoritative, biblical, and historically orthodox answer to that essential question "Who do we say that Jesus is?" The essays contained in this book are the edited addresses given at this conference.

This conference, like other Anglican Institute conferences (The Practice of Anglicanism [1993], The Reconstruction of a Vital Via Media [1994], Unashamed Anglicanism [1996], The Bible [1998], The Hope of Heaven [1999], all in Colorado Springs, Colorado, and The Truth About Jesus [1997], held in Birmingham, Alabama), had as its purpose the promotion of a vibrant, historic Christianity in the Anglican Tradition. The impressive list of contributors to this volume indicates the wide-ranging and serious efforts of the Institute to consider topics of core importance to the life of faith. By bringing together the finest minds in the church it has been and will continue to be our goal to offer a forum for significant theological reflection for the clergy and lay members of the church.

In an age of chaos and uncertainty, both in the church and in the culture, an effective faith grounded in a sturdy tradition is desperately needed. The Institute, not politically engaged in the ever-changing and symptomatic temporal issues, is positioned to help reclaim the church's historic identity and spiritual focus that it may be the vehicle for the mighty works of God.

We believe in grounding our work in those formational historic events of the incarnation, crucifixion, resurrection of Christ, and the coming of the Holy Spirit combined with the tolerance, fair-mindedness, and generosity which have long marked our Anglican way. It is simply the apostolic Christian faith — expressed in Scripture, interpreted in the creeds, guarded by tradition and experienced in sacrament — that we wish to fortify and proclaim.

The special nature of the conference of which this book is the result required significant support to produce. I particularly want to thank Bill & Genie Armstrong, Dick & Sally Bean, Jane Black, Bryan & Amy Carr, Laura Clemens, Bess Duff, Fred & Rebecca Eberbach, Creswell Fleming, Chuck Fogleman, Libby Fordyce, A. M. Fowler-Mayer, Jack & Becky Gloriod, Ebe & Evie Liddle, Jim & Phyllis Moore, Jo Ann Platt, Jane Rouse, Andy Schumacher, Ann & Hugh Scott, Lew Shepley, Rudy & Gordon Shouse, Jack Singleton, Edith Spink, Bill & Bette Storms, Elsie Valier, Bud & Barbara Weir, Harold Whitney, Kay Wiese, and John & Jan Williams for their timely and generous contributions. Without their help, encouragement, and faith this conference could not have taken place and this important volume would not have been produced. I also want to thank the Episcopal Church Women and the Vestry of Grace & St. Stephen's Episcopal Church in Colorado Springs, the Vestry of St. Francis Episcopal Church in Potomac, Maryland, and its Rector, the Rev. William Shands, and the Chapter of the Cathedral Church of the Advent in Birmingham, Alabama, and its Dean, the Very Rev. Dr. Paul F. M. Zahl, for their significant financial support and commitment to this project.

The setting for this conference in Paris, France, encouraged a diverse and international participation. The gracious ministry of hospitality offered by the cathedral guilds, clergy and office staff, its Dean, the Very Rev. Dr. Ernest Hunt, and the Bishop of the Convocation of American Churches in Europe, the Rt. Rev. Jeffrey Rowthorn, reflected the splendid and extensive ministry of this great cathedral of the Episcopal Church. Of particular importance to the shape, character, and experience of a conference such as this is the experience of worship. The words of the mind became heartfelt truth in the worship led by the Rev. Canon Nicholas Porter, sung by the cathedral choir under the direction of Canon Precentor Edward Tipton, assisted by Edward Hughes.

Of particular importance to this conference, following so soon after the Lambeth Conference of 1998, was the enthusiastic and scholarly preaching of the Bishop of the Rift Valley, Tanzania, East Africa, the Rt. Rev. Alpha Mohammed.

A special thanks must be given to Jackson & Betty Gouraud whose generosity, participation, and counsel has been a significant factor enabling The Institute to greatly expand the effectiveness and reach of its work. Their presence at each Anglican Institute conference and continued support and wisdom between conferences is an invaluable asset to this ministry. I also wish to again thank the Rev. Dr. Alister McGrath for his theological advice and counsel in the design and substance of all our Anglican Institute conferences and projects. And lastly I wish to express love and praise to Institute Administrator Jessie Armstrong, whose tireless efforts and balanced perspective keep the whole enterprise viable and on course.

The Rev. Donald Armstrong
Institute Rector

Introduction

In our current time, the essential and life-changing question that Jesus asked of his disciples, "Who do you say that I am?" has been, in the theology of many, effectively changed to "Who would you like me to be?" From radical feminist theologians who critique Jesus through their particular experience as women to church growth experts who offer "God at your service," Jesus has been revisioned and reimaged to bless what we have become and grant the fulfillment of our excessive desires.

Many, in their religious searching, have been seduced by a hermeneutic of self-centeredness and self-glorification. In this theory of interpretation and search for meaning we produce theological doctrine by backing into it. We start with ourselves and then re-image God to match what we would do if we were the Creator, rather than the creatures we seem to have forgotten we are. We use a supermarket approach for finding a place of worship in which we shop for the God of our choosing, not to bless and sanctify us, but to approve and justify us. God on my terms, in my image, and at my service is the demand of postmodern seekers.

The stern and tender God, described by Tom Wright in his contribution to this volume, who is relentlessly opposed to all that destroys or distorts human beings, but at the same time recklessly loving all those in need and distress, has been replaced by a celestial bellhop, a mirror, mirror on the wall telling us that we, in whatever form we have become, are the fairest of all.

A recent candidate for Bishop in the Episcopal Church responded to a question on this subject by stating: "the Holy Spirit is now speaking to certain individuals in the church to correct the mistakes in the revelation of God in Christ as recorded in the culturally conditioned and totally incomplete metaphors of Holy Scripture." H. Richard Niebuhr's prediction in *The Kingdom of God in America* that we might soon embrace "a God without wrath bringing men without sin into a kingdom without judgement through the ministrations of a Christ without a cross" is clearly coming to pass. This misguided and misinformed theological position is held, not only by those occupying an occasional seat in the pew, but by many charged with the protection and proclamation of the apostolic truth.

It is the purpose of this book to articulate and make accessible a credible antidote to this devastating, despairing, and inaccurate picture of God. The concern that led to the conference, which is the content of this book, was not merely that some people have bad theology, that others are following their own noses instead of Jesus Christ, and that a theology of blessing has been converted into a theology of permission. It is that this new image of Jesus, which finds its source not in Scripture and tradition, but in human narcissism, is quickly becoming the basis for a new religion that supplants the faith of the apostles, takes the name of Christianity, and resides unchallenged in our churches. Somehow and somewhere the classic faith of the apostles needs to be clearly and decisively articulated and applied to the current situation. It is our intention and hope that this volume will accomplish precisely that task.

It is my further hope that through the excellent papers herein presented, rather than re-visioning Jesus in our image and likeness, we might meet him afresh and be ourselves reimaged in his likeness.

The Rev. Dr. Christopher Hancock offers precisely this possibility in his opening paper "The Christological Problem," where he suggests that the question isn't so much about what we make of Jesus as what he makes of us and what God has to say to us in Jesus. Quoting Martin Luther, Dr. Hancock says that the christological problem becomes the personally appropriated christocentric life when we can claim that "Jesus is *my* Lord and *my* God and He died for *me*. He has gone to prepare a place *for me* and will be there on the other side of *my* death." Here is the God that we might dwell in him and he in us.

The Rev. Dr. Richard Reid in his presentation, "The Necessity of a Biblical Christology," claims that to encounter the true and living God one must have as their source and definition the revelation of Holy Scripture which provides the only real access we have to the person of Jesus. Not only does the Scripture provide us with information about him, it also interprets that information and helps us to understand its significance. Dr. Reid argues that "Christology which is not rooted in the Bible — which does not take into account the context, and the content, and the continuity which the Bible provides, will always be inadequate, or worse, just plain wrong. It may even turn Christianity into a different religion altogether."

In "The Biblical Formation of a Doctrine of Christ," The Rev. Dr. N. T. Wright underscores the urgency for the church to answer the christological inquiry. He argues that the church's true mission will begin to be accomplished as we discover more and more who Jesus was and is precisely in order that we as a church and as individual followers of Jesus be equipped to engage the world that he came to save. "The mission of the church," he says, "can be summed up in the phrase 'reflected glory,' . . . that [God's] glory may shine in us and through us, to bring light and life to a world that still waits in darkness and in the shadow of death."

The Rev. Dr. Alister McGrath, in his chapter "Christology: On Learning from History," suggests that part of our Anglican heritage lies in a willingness to take the past seriously, and avoid "the sheer arrogance of those who assert that all those unfortunate enough to live before 1950 were doomed to superstition and ignorance." "A willingness to listen to the past," writes Dr. McGrath, "and even to learn from it, comes hard to those who stridently dismiss the past because they fear what such an engagement might yield." Challenging the ill-conceived notion "that the present is, by definition, more enlightened than the past," he identifies the lessons to be learned from it, and embarks on the liberation of Jesus from the bonds which Western thinking has placed upon him. Shining in and through this essay is the Jesus of Scripture and tradition who died for the sins of the *whole* world.

In his presentation, *The Biblical Christ in a Pagan Culture*, Mr. Alan Crippen calls for the end of parochialism, not that we become resident aliens, but that we might become soldiers with an invasion strategy. He says we are to be the church militant on the way to becoming the church triumphant. We are God's salvation army of occupation in this world. The mission of local parishes is to reorder their cultural life in anticipation of the coming new world order.

The Most Rev. and Rt. Hon. George L. Carey concludes in his presentation *Christ and His Church* that the perceptions of the church as bureaucracy, as institutionalized morality, as social agency, as the school of liberal humanism, must be challenged and changed. The Archbishop calls for these models to be "replaced with a model of the church as the sacrament of Christ, of his incarnate nature, and of his act of gratuitous love for the world in his Cross and Resurrection." Such a change would be costly and disturbing, for, says Dr. Carey, "The Church can only become this sacramental sign if it gives itself unreservedly to living and proclaiming Christ as Lord and Hope of Glory." Dr. Carey challenges us to take Christ deeply into every aspect of our lives and ministry and community, that we might walk confidently with the gospel of Christ as members of a Christ-like church; "a church worth belonging to — because it truly, and authentically, belongs to him."

As one reads these chapters, it becomes unarguably clear that it is only in the Jesus revealed in the Holy Scripture, experienced in the tradition of liturgical worship, and upheld in the doctrine and discipline of the church, that we can know who and whose we ultimately are. Jesus said: "If you continue in my word, you are truly my disciples; and you will know the truth, and the truth will make you free." And the truth is that Jesus is "the Messiah, the Son of the living God." With this truth as our answer to the question "Who do you say that I am?" closely held in hearts and minds, we can live in God's world, on God's terms, in the hope of God's heaven.

Shrove Tuesday, 1999
Colorado Springs, Colorado

The Rev. Donald Armstrong
Institute Rector

The Christological Problem

CHRISTOPHER D. HANCOCK

So, once again, for the last time or the first, we face that face . . .

FREDERICK BUECHNER

I have been asked to consider the formidable subject, *"the christo-logical problem."* This subject addresses the heart of the Christian faith. I am mindful of C. S. Lewis's warning to scholars, "If you can't turn your faith into the vernacular, then either you don't understand it or you don't believe it." In dealing with such a large topic, the artist Vincent Van Gogh's advice to his brother Theo is also pertinent, "Exaggerate the essentials; leave the rest vague." The aim of this chapter is, in the words of the Epistle to the Hebrews, to "consider Him," to "fix our eyes on Jesus, the author and perfecter of our faith" (12:2, 3).

Looking back at lecture notes for courses on Christology that I've taught over the years at Virginia Theological Seminary I found these words: "I approach teaching 'The Person and Work of Christ' with more hesitancy, more circumspection, more self-examination and with greater self-criticism with each succeeding year." Those were the words of an academic; now as a parish priest I'm more than ever committed to their truth. For pastoral ministry and theological reflection together confirm that Christology — that is, faithful reflection on the history, identity, personality, and significance of Jesus Christ — is not *a* problem, but, to the eye of faith, *the* problem posed by God to the world. It encompasses the supreme question and the supreme answer in life. It isn't so much about what we make of Jesus as what he makes of us. For Jesus is, as Emil Brunner wrote, "what God has to say to us." The study of Jesus Christ, Christology, is an invitation to an intellectual, a spiritual, and an eternal feast hosted by God, served by Christ, and enlivened by God's Spirit.

I have organized this introductory chapter for this volume around seven key issues for different types of inquirers.

1. The Problem of Christology for the Diligent Student

At the end of the first chapter of John McIntyre's book *The Shape of Christology* (1966) we read these words:

> If we define Christology as rational reflection upon the person, nature and claims of him with whom we have to do when we make the confession, 'I believe in the Lord Jesus Christ', then in the process of such analysis the simple given reveals itself to be an amazing complexity.[1]

Notice that phrase, "the simple given reveals itself to be an amazing complexity." A subject of amazing complexity confronts the student of Christology. Study of any person is a complex business — let alone someone claiming and believed to be God, and venerated for two thousand years in many languages, cultures, crises, and contexts. Biography, theology, psychology, spirituality, philosophy, sociology, ecclesiology, sacramental theology, comparative religion, all impinge on the mind and heart of the diligent student of Christology.

In 1989 the editor and translator for SCM, John Bowden, published a book entitled *Jesus: The Unanswered Questions*. I quote from it to illustrate this first point, viz. *the complexity of Christology*.

1. John McIntyre, *The Shape of Christology* (London: SCM Press, 1966), 26.

This is a book of questions. They arise out of a wide variety of areas of Christian thought, practice and experience: study of the Bible, doctrine, ethics, the history of Christianity, liturgy, personal prayer, pastoral work, the use of Christian belief as a source of manipulation within society and the relationship between Christianity and other faiths — to mention the main ones. Few of these questions are ones that I have thought up myself; some are more sophisticated than others, but they can all be found elsewhere, often discussed at great length.[2]

Later he adds,

The questions are all focussed on Jesus, because on any account Jesus of Nazareth, and the developments to which he gave rise, are the focal points of Christianity, and it is around the interpretation of his person, Christology, that so many problems cluster.[3]

A direct corollary of *the complexity of Christology* for the diligent student is *the plurality of perspectives* found — and I don't just mean the mountain of literature that, broadly speaking, deals with Christology.

To illustrate this, we return to McIntyre's *The Shape of Christology*. In chapter two, McIntyre identifies eight "methods" in Christology. We take these to represent eight different perspectives on "the christological problem." The list isn't exhaustive, but it is a useful starting point.

   i. *The dogmatic method,* which comes to the New Testament account of Jesus Christ with clear dogmatic presuppositions, shaped by the historic faith of the church;
   ii. *The historical method,* which critically cross-examines the historical evidence for the person and work of Jesus Christ, questioning the verifiability or falsifiability of Christology's historical records (e.g. the New Testament);

2. John Bowden, *Jesus: The Unanswered Questions* (Nashville: Abingdon Press, 1989), xiii.
3. Bowden, *Jesus,* xv.

iii. *The literary-critical method,* which examines the meaning of words and the status of texts *qua* texts dealing with Jesus of Nazareth (as a subcategory of this we might add now *the deconstructionist method,* with its suspicion of textual meaning or commitment to an infinite plurality of meanings in texts);

iv. *The mediatory method,* which, McIntyre argues, seeks to release into the present the meaning and reality of Christ's person and work from the history and texts about him;

v. *The "singular" method,* which ascribes a radical singularity to the Christ-event and rejects its accountability to the constraints of scientific inquiry and certain forms of historical exegesis;

vi. *The socio-geographic method,* with its preoccupation with understanding Jesus in his humanity in a particular time, place, and cultural context (under this heading we might gather today literature on "Jesus the Jew" or writing associated with the "Second" or "Third" "Quest for the Historical Jesus");

vii. *The liturgical method,* which sees the foundation and fulfillment of christological reflection in the dynamic context of liturgy, worship, and preaching;

viii. *The ethical method,* which, according to McIntyre, looks at Jesus Christ as a paradigm or principle of moral integrity in the vicarious conformity of his life to the will and purpose of God.

Though couched in generalities these eight perspectives address fundamental issues in Christology. In particular, they ask, What does the church say about Jesus? Can the Gospels be trusted? What do Jesus' life and death mean for us today? What does it mean to claim uniqueness for Jesus? What kind of man was he? How can or should someone respond to him? What does his life say about living today? McIntyre's eight perspectives (and others we might add) explain the volume and variety of material comprising "the christological problem" which confront the diligent student.

2. The Problem of Christology for the Honest Scholar

Changing tack, I want to move from the problems of Christology for the student to those of the scholar; to shift, that is, from the stance of a spectator to that of a participant. What problems confront the person who is willing to participate actively and intellectually in the quest to understand Jesus?

At the beginning of chapter one of David Wells's helpful introduction to Christology, entitled *The Person of Christ*, we read this:

> The shape which our Christology assumes is determined by the presuppositions and operating assumptions with which we start.[4]

It's a frank and honest admission that behind the complexity and plurality of perspectives on Jesus Christ lies a host of scholarly presuppositions that give shape and character to a Christologian's inquiry and conclusions. Wells lists three pervasive presuppositions that shape the way the christological problem is often addressed:

- first, *literary presuppositions* about how the Bible should be analyzed and used;
- secondly, *intellectual presuppositions* — that is, philosophical or epistemological decisions about what can or cannot be accepted now in the late twentieth century about what could or could not happen in the first century as recorded in the Gospels (N.B. debates about Jesus' miracles fall into this category, as do the equally complex issues of exorcism, sexual purity, and the nature of "wholeness" in humanity);
- thirdly, *interpretative or hermeneutic presuppositions* — "categories of understanding," he calls them — that is, explicitly named filters through which data dealing with Jesus is both discerned and disseminated.

4. David Wells, *The Person of Christ* (London: Marshall, Morgan & Scott, 1984), 21.

In illustration of this third category, Wells cites the *Lives of Jesus* written by the nineteenth-century German Friedrich Schleiermacher and the twentieth-century American Shirley Jackson Case. Both strip Jesus of supernaturalism. They illustrate the pungency of interpretative presuppositions for Christology. As Wells observes,

> The supernatural was 'reinterpreted', the uniqueness of Jesus being concentrated under the thought of the mystery of his personality, the power of his morality, or the sublimity of his teaching. Such a teacher was, in fact, no different from any other great leader and teacher, and the faith he taught was generically no different from the other great religions of the world.

Wells asks of this non-supernaturalist filter (or "category of understanding"),

> Does this reinterpretation really do justice to the figure at the focus of the Gospel accounts? Do we not have here what Bultmann called disparagingly 'a middle class conception of Christianity', and one which is quite out of touch with 'the strangeness of the New Testament'?[5]

Wells alerts us to the extent to which a scholar's — indeed, our own — understanding of Jesus Christ is consciously, or unconsciously, conditional upon a range of potential or actual presuppositions. To say that is *not* to say that presuppositions are necessarily wrong. It is to understand that presuppositions in Christology are both inevitable and (potentially, at least) identifiable. In Christology (as in theology, generally), where you begin shapes where you end. Christology flourishes when it honestly faces this fact.

I want to address briefly now two further issues under this second heading:

a. If it's true presuppositions shape Christology, the question remains, *"Are there more or less appropriate presuppositions for Christology?"* Or, to focus the question more precisely still, *"Is Christology best done by (what used to be called) 'the alienated theologian' (the one who*

---

5. Wells, *Person of Christ*, 21.

claims neutrality of conviction concerning Jesus) or 'the invested theologian'
(who makes no bones about being a professing believer)?"

Not so long ago detachment was commended.[6] More recently, a committed or "invested" stance in sociology, epistemology, and ecclesiology has been reaccredited. Commitment permits the inquirer to pursue a subject freely, radically, singularly, where the subject leads. The word *christ-ology* itself suggests commitment. It evokes the sense that there is more to Jesus than mere history. Indeed, christological "commitment" to Jesus — as both subject and object — acknowledges his preeminence both as theme (to control inquiry) and as person (to challenge presuppositions). The "invested" stance is both epistemologically necessary and spiritually appropriate. Apart from this commitment the subject Jesus Christ cannot be said to shape christological inquiry nor lead christological discovery. With this investment Christology assumes a new level of honest self-criticism (for it is accountable to *this* figure, Jesus) and a new kind of self-awareness (cross-examining the propriety of presuppositions it employs). The fruit of "invested" Christology is a presuppositional commitment to Jesus Christ as both historical fact *and* spiritual figure, as significant both phenomenologically *and* theologically. This represents the irreducible core of honest scholarly commitment to "the christological problem." In the light of this Christology we can consider aright the radical claims, unique character, and ultimate significance of Jesus of Nazareth.

b. Following on from this, christological inquiry must be *dynamic*. In this, it is not unlike any *living* subject; though now, in a particular way, this subject (if indeed *the living Christ*) must be permitted to dominate inquiry with his own dynamic freedom to pull, push, shape, elude, as always greater, always free. As in any *worthy* subject — only more so, if the subject is worthy of worship — control is, as we've seen already, surrendered by the scholar or worshipper to this figure, Christ. Understanding and interpretation are to be seen

---

6. See the discussion in Van Austin Harvey, *The Historian and the Believer: The Morality of Historical Knowledge and Christian Belief* (Philadelphia: Westminster, 1966), 68-163; and his article, "The Alienated Theologian" in *McCormick Quarterly* 23 (May 1970): 234f.

then as dynamically *given* (like divine revelation), not presumptuously *grasped* (by critical scholarship). The Anglo-Catholic theologian E. L. Mascall makes an important christological and ecclesiological application of this when he writes in his book *Jesus: Who He is and How We Know Him,*

> That the Christ whom we know today is the historic Christ, is basic to our faith, but we do not depend for our acquaintance with Him on the research of historians and archaeologists. He is also the heavenly Christ, and as such is the object (we might say, the subject) of our present experience, mediated through the sacramental life of the Church.[7]

In other words, the honest Christologian (who surrenders control to Jesus as subject) has reckoned with the dynamic greatness of the living, reigning, dominating figure of Christ. Considering Christ, she looks up to Christ, and is confronted by her lack of faith and limitation in understanding. Dietrich Bonhoeffer expressed his own sense of this inner, rhetorical dynamism in Christology when he spoke of Jesus Christ as the great *questioner* of humanity. Writing in his *Letters and Papers from Prison* he poignantly comments, "What is bothering me incessantly is the question what Christianity really is, or indeed who Christ really is, for us today."[8] We would do well to face the fact, like Bonhoeffer, that the historical Jesus and the dynamic, sovereign Christ is a botherer, and good Christology a bothersome, questioning kind of thing!

3. The Problem of Christology for the Critical Skeptic

So much, then, for the problem of Christology for the diligent student and honest scholar. Does Christology present any kind of prob-

---

7. Edward L. Mascall, *Jesus: Who He Is and How We Know Him* (London: Darton, Longman & Todd, 1985), 38-39.

8. Dietrich Bonhoeffer, letter to E. Bethge, 30 April 1944, *Letters and Papers from Prison,* revised and enlarged edition (London: SCM Press, 1971), 279.

lem for those who are skeptical about its significance, submerged (perhaps) in ignorance, or critical of its relevance? It is all very well to address the christological problem as it pertains to those "in the know" within the circle of faith; but, is that a sufficient account of the one who reached out to the nocturnal Nicodemus and confronted the skeptical Thomas? Christology that cannot be bothered with, or bother a little, the critical skeptic is not worthy of the name. True Christology is as much the art of communicating Christ to a skeptical world as it is the science of understanding him in the context of faith. So what of the problem of Christology for the critical skeptic?

One of the most pressing problems Christology presents to the skeptic or cynic is, I would argue, *the lingering aura of Christ's radiant character.* After two thousand years very few disparage Jesus' greatness or question his goodness. In my experience of evangelism and pastoral ministry I am yet to meet someone who needs persuading Jesus was "a good man": this conviction may not lead to faith, but it is a good place to start. Many times I have quoted the poet Tennyson's description of Jesus' character as "more wonderful than the greatest miracle," and J. S. Mills's description of him as "a unique figure, not more unlike all His predecessors than all His followers." I even quote, if I have it to hand, this statement I found one day by P. Carnegie Simpson:

> Instinctively we do not class Him with others. When one reads His name in a list beginning with Confucius and ending with Goethe we feel it is an offence less against orthodoxy than against decency. Jesus is not one of the group of the world's great. Talk about Alexander the Great and Charles the Great and Napoleon the Great, if you will . . . Jesus is apart. He is not the Great; He is the Only. He is simply Jesus.

Simpson may press some skeptics too far. But I have found many over the years who have responded, as he puts it, "instinctively" to Jesus's greatness. They have felt with Charles Lamb that, "If Shakespeare were to come into the room we would all rise up to greet him, but if Jesus Christ were to enter we would fall on our knees and seek to kiss the hem of His garment." This is the *lingering aura* surrounding Jesus Christ. As James Denney wrote memorably in *Jesus and the Gospel,*

9

From beginning to end, in all its various phases and aspects and elements, the Christian faith and life is determined by Jesus Christ. It owes its life and character at every point to Him. Its convictions are convictions about Him. Its hopes are hopes which He has inspired, and which it is for Him to fulfil. Its ideals are born from His teaching and His life. Its strength is the strength of His spirit.[9]

If not a spiritual, theological, or even historical problem for the skeptic, Jesus Christ is a lingering *cultural* problem. As Jaroslav Pelikan points out in *Jesus Through the Centuries: His Place in the History of Culture:*

For each age, the life and teaching of Jesus represented an answer (or, more often, *the* answer) to the most fundamental questions of human existence and of human destiny, and it was to the figure of Jesus as set forth in the Gospels that those questions were addressed.[10]

To both the diligent student and the honest scholar the lingering aura and cultural awareness of Jesus Christ's character and work provide invaluable grist to the christological mill. Culture, if not Scripture, echoes Jesus' question to the skeptical unbeliever: "Who do you say that I am?" The figure of Jesus in art and literature, in music and drama, keeps alive "the christological problem" beyond the circle of faith.

My wife Suzie and I saw this clearly after a Japanese student living with us returned from a weekend visiting the art galleries of Paris. In the course of a meal she suddenly asked — drawing a cross on the table — "What does this mean? And why did the man have those injuries?" It is tempting to think the case for Christ stands or falls on the witness of Scripture or the skillfulness of a theological author: no, the most eloquent account may arise from popular cultural portraiture.

---

9. James Denney, *Jesus and the Gospel* (Cincinnati: Jennings & Graham, 1910), 1.

10. Jaroslav Pelikan, *Jesus Through the Centuries* (New York: Harper & Row, 1985), 2.

4. The Problem of Christology for the New Testament Reader

However potent cultural influence (for good and ill) on understanding Jesus Christ (after all, to quote Jaroslav Pelikan once again, Jesus has been "the dominant figure in the history of Western culture for almost twenty centuries"), to come "face to face" with him leads us to the problem of Christology for the New Testament reader. Sooner or later "the christological problem" is an *exegetical* problem. The New Testament Gospels are the primary textual cause and abiding literary companion of all responsible christological reflection. But what problems do they present us with?

Other chapters will address the biblical christological literature in greater detail. I restrict myself to three general comments of an introductory kind. They concern the parameters of a reader's expectations of the biblical literature.

Firstly, the Gospels may be said to provide a *sufficient resource* for Christology. That is, they provide *sufficient* information for a reader to know the basic *facts* of Jesus' life and the essential *acts* whereby he saves. Article VI of Anglicanism's Thirty-nine Articles of Religion addresses this, maintaining that Scripture "contains all things necessary unto salvation." In other words, the New Testament provides *enough* to profess faith that this Jesus is God's Christ. It is the primary source for knowledge about Jesus and the primary literary resource for faith in him as Christ. It is the starting point historically, exegetically, theologically, and spiritually for reflection on Jesus Christ. It is *sufficient* in that at the outset of christological reflection no additional information is necessary and in the communication of Christ's work of salvation no supplementary data or work is essential. Leaving aside issues of infallibility, inerrancy (and even accuracy), this is simply to say, "Here there is *enough*."

Secondly, the Gospels provide an *authoritative source* for Christology. A direct corollary to claiming *sufficiency* for the New Testament is affirmation of its christological *authority*. But let's be clear: the authoritative, canonical status of the New Testament Gospels rests — as Article VII of the Thirty-nine Articles makes clear — not on some human decision to accredit certain texts but on the unique manner in which they bear witness to a unique figure, a unique savior. As Article VII states:

> Both in the Old and New Testament everlasting life is offered to mankind by Christ, who is the only mediator between God and man.

Commenting on this Oliver O'Donovan wisely explains,

> . . . the authority of Jesus and of these events (recorded in the Gospels) is (from an epistemological point of view) vested entirely in the New Testament, and communicated exclusively through its witness. There is no other route by which these events make themselves known to later generations.[11]

In other words, the uniquely authoritative character of the Gospels and the unique figure they portray are inseparable. In the end, the diligent student, the honest scholar, and the critical skeptic are brought to the bar of Scripture. Here thought and study are provoked, presuppositions formed and challenged, doubt addressed and faith inspired.

Thirdly, the New Testament Gospels provide a *narrative force* within Christology. It is possible to overstate problems in understanding or using the gospel account of Jesus. To a reasonable reader, the problem is *not* that the Gospels do *not* tell one story about one person in four ways: the problem is they *do*. Again, the problem for the New Testament reader (with or without faith) is *not* the obscurity of the gospel narrative, nor its predictable biographical and chronological diversity, but its remarkable clarity and unity given its antiquity. Furthermore, surely, the problem for the reader is *not* that the Gospels say too little about unimportant things but so much about extremely important things. Though scholars may get lost in details, to storytellers and story-readers the Gospels have amazing narrative force: they drive Christology.

---

11. Oliver O'Donovan, *On the Thirty-Nine Articles: A Conversation with Tudor Christianity* (Exeter: Paternoster Press, 1986), 51.

The narrative force of the canonical Gospels constitutes the essential cause of which Christian faith and two thousand years of church history are the remarkable effects. What is more, as *story,* the medium of story should, I suggest, continue to form the genre in which the Gospels are read and interpreted and the focus through which the rest of the New Testament is given coherence and contemporary relevance.

So much for my three general introductory thoughts. I ought to come clean and explain why I have included them. In part, because (to an Anglican!) they express a classical Anglican biblical hermeneutic, which is both christocentric and coherent. In part, also (and, possibly more importantly) because they express the epistemological principle articulated previously. According to this, the subject of an inquiry (here Jesus in the Gospels) should have priority, freedom, and power over the reader. The text and its subject, to be treated responsibly, always hold the initiative. In this way manipulation of the content of the biblical data (by overt or covert presuppositional assumptions) and evasion of the impact of the biblical figure (Jesus Christ) can be held in check. This hermeneutic principle does justice both to Jesus and the Gospels.

Recent reflection on the role of texts *qua* texts suggests that part of the problem of Christology for the New Testament reader lies in reckoning with the determinative historic function of the biblical narrative in the formation of the Christian community. Texts which tell the story of Jesus have forged and formed the faith and life of the church. They have been accorded power and authority to grasp, shake, push and pull (and bother!) both the reader and the church. Doubts linger about the details of Jesus' life. Little doubt surrounds the historic, christological role of the Bible in the life of the church. Over the centuries the church has confidently affirmed the Gospels' power to bring the reader "face to face" with Jesus. Through them we meet him — and meet him together. We meet the one whose "cast of mind" was (as Dodd records)[12] original, intelligent, creative, sensitive, imaginative, picto-

12. Cf. Charles H. Dodd, *The Founder of Christianity* (Glasgow: William Collins, 1971), chapters 3 and 4.

rial, concrete, cryptic, ironic, humorous, mystical, allusive. We meet one whose manner was sociable, bold, bracing, sympathetic, forgiving, single-minded, friendly, authoritative, rugged, deliberate, thoughtful, encouraging, devout, reserved, solitary. This is Jesus. This is the biblical figure at the heart of Western culture. The problem for the New Testament reader is "Who on earth is he?" It was the problem Jesus' contemporaries faced. It's the heart of the christological problem today. It's *the* question longing for an answer.

5. The Problem of Christology for the Historian of Doctrine

A good case can, I believe, be made for the possibility of a New Testament reader coming "face to face" with Jesus. Biblical studies and historical theology reveal, however, both doubters and disciples struggling with the question "Who on earth is he?" The history of their struggle to answer that question is central to the problem of Christology for the historian of doctrine.

Rather than attempt the impossible task of reviewing the history of christological thought, let me suggest that the problem of Christology for the historian of doctrine consists of four key issues: the divinity of Christ, the development of doctrine, the role of culture, and the impact of science. A brief comment on each.

a. *The divinity of Christ.* The existence and humanity of Jesus are unquestioned by the writers of the New Testament. Biblical studies and the history of doctrine grapple with "the more" claimed by the carpenter's son, his contemporaries and successors. The New Testament, the earliest creeds and first five ecumenical councils of the church reflect progressive reflection on the identity of Jesus and growing confidence in his divinity as Son of God. Progressive reflection is already apparent in the Gospels, as Vincent Taylor points out in his classic study *The Person of Christ:*

> The development which can be seen [in the Gospels] is not a mark of corruption, but a process of interpretation made necessary as

14

the tradition is understood better and is expounded in the light of the missionary expansion of the primitive Church.[13]

In the process of according full, or true, divinity to Jesus Christ (*pace* the Council of Nicaea in 325 AD) prayer, worship, preaching, evangelism, and hardheaded philosophical reflection all had a place. The path from Peter's confession "You are the Christ" — via the Logos Christologies of John and Philo and the subordinationism of Origen and Arius — to Nicaea's "Christ is not made, being of one substance with the Father" was directed by the twin concern to honor the indivisibility of divinity *and* the mystery of incarnation. Nicaea left open the door to Apollinarius's denial of Jesus Christ's full humanity. Apollinarius argued that the divine Logos replaced the human spirit and will in Jesus. The incarnate Person had a human body, a human soul, but a *divine* Spirit, he maintained. The Council of Constantinople (381 AD) judged Apollinarius heretical, claiming that only one who is fully God and fully man can fully save and fully sympathize.

Following Constantinople, the Antiochene school (led by Nestorius) challenged the unity of Christ's "person" and the monk Pelagius the sufficiency of Christ's "work." Nestorius argued for two distinct, but essentially unrelated, "natures"; Pelagius for human "free will" in salvation. Both were condemned at the Council of Ephesus (431 AD) where Cyril of Alexandria and Augustine affirmed the God-Man Jesus Christ to be *one* person and the perfect savior. The Council of Chalcedon (451 AD), opposing as it did Eutyches' claim that there were two natures before the incarnation and one after, established the definitive "Definition" of incarnational orthodoxy. Chalcedon held that the one Lord Jesus Christ is both God and Man, one person in two natures. The subsequent history of christological thought is the history of the church's attempts to own, refine, reconstruct, and reformulate Chalcedon's "two nature Christology" (as it is called) and where necessary repudiate its rejection.

The problem of Christology for the historian of doctrine con-

13. Vincent Taylor, *The Person of Christ* (London: Macmillan, 1958), 22-23.

cerns originally, then, the church's progressive affirmation of full divinity in Jesus Christ, and its relation to his humanity.

b. *The development of doctrine.* The history of christological reflection is inseparable from the history and critique of doctrinal development in the church. New Testament scholars chart development through Scripture, theologians through history. Pressure of a positive and negative kind inside and outside the church fuelled the fires of controversy. Internally, the church struggled to find and defend intelligible ways of communicating Christ to alien cultures (theologians in the East and West disagreed about the value of secular thought in apologetics). Externally, the church encountered a plethora of intellectual and religious traditions and practices that shaped or corrupted Christology. Platonism, Hellenism, Judaism, gnosticism, mystery religions and cultic acts variously influenced Christian theology and worship. To the late nineteenth-century German church historian Adolf von Harnack this influence was almost entirely corrosive. Writing in his *History of Dogma,* Harnack argued that the origin of dogma lay "in the activity of the Hellenic spirit upon the gospel soil." As he wrote in volume seven,

> The gospel entered into the world, not as a doctrine, but as a joyful message and as a power of the Spirit of God, originally in the forms of Judaism. It stripped off these forms with amazing rapidity, and united and amalgamated itself with Greek science, the Roman Empire, and ancient culture.[14]

To Harnack, the historian of doctrine must guide the church to strip off the "husk" of cultural accretion from the "kernel" of gospel truth. The "Chalcedonian Definition," for example, must be jettisoned "in order that the gospel might be preserved." The French scholar Alfred Loisy[15] countered Harnack at the time. Subsequent defenders of the normativity of the Bible, the ecumenical creeds, or the *magisterium* of the church have likewise repudiated Harnack's

---

14. Adolf von Harnack, *The History of Dogma,* vol. 7 (Edinburgh: Williams & Norgate, 1894-1899), 272.

15. Cf. Alfred Loisy, *The Gospel and the Church* (1903; Philadelphia: Fortress Press, 1976).

critique of doctrinal development. But Harnack is an influential voice in support of all who have heard Jesus' question, "Who do you say that I am?" and challenged the character and content of the church's original answers.

c. *The role of culture.* As we see above, culture plays a major part in Christology. It has done so for good and ill from the beginning. H. Richard Niebuhr's modern classic *Christ and Culture* (1951)[16] fuelled mid-century debates. To Niebuhr the issue was not how culture encountered Christianity but how Christ encountered culture. Following Bonhoeffer, Niebuhr asked not, Who? but, Where? (is Jesus Christ in our world). Is Christ against culture or within it? Is he Lord over it or the transformer of it? In many ways Niebuhr reprised patristic debate about the role of secular thought. Recently, "Liberation Theology" and creative indigenous Christologies (imaging the creative missionary theologizing of Roland Allen) have taken discussions further. These have proved controversial. Caution is certainly needed. Culture can be corrosive of classical, biblical Christology. But this comment of Vincent Taylor on christological development in the New Testament is helpful:

> The development which can be seen is not a mark of corruption [*pace* Harnack] but a process of interpretation made necessary as the tradition is understood better and is expounded in the light of the missionary expansion of the primitive church.[17]

Christology plus culture do not necessarily equal corruption. Indeed, to be worthy of its name Christology takes culture seriously. It cannot and must not be denied. After all, the Christ of whom Christology speaks is the universal, *cosmic* Christ; and the God of Jesus Christ "loved *the world* so much that he sent his only-begotten Son."[18]

d. *The impact of science.* The historian of Christology cannot overlook the impact of the natural and social sciences on Christian

16. Cf. H. Richard Niebuhr, *Christ and Culture* (New York: Harper & Row, 1951).

17. Taylor, *Person of Christ*, 22-23.

18. John 3:16.

reflection on the person and work of Christ. Back in 1950 W. R. Matthews, then Dean of St. Paul's Cathedral in London, published a slight volume entitled, *The Problem of Christ in the Twentieth Century*. In it he identifies three pressing problems for the church's understanding of Jesus at the time:

i. *Historical inquiry* (or "criticism" of New Testament evidence for Jesus) — calling for reformulation of the doctrine of the incarnation because "we know practically nothing about the real Jesus";[19]

ii. *The nineteenth-century heritage* — critiquing (*pace* Friedrich Schleiermacher) the theological and linguistic adequacy of the christological terms "nature" and "person" and affirming (*pace* Albrecht Ritschl) the importance of ethical/historical value judgments about Jesus;[20]

iii. *Twentieth-century developments in psychology (and philosophy)* — i.e. the work of Jung, Rhine, Myers, Sanday, and Tyrrell as it pertains to understanding Jesus' will, behavior, and personality.[21]

According to Matthews, scientific discovery (in this instance psychology) requires a fresh appraisal of classic "two nature" Christologies. Traditional theories of the person and work of Christ fail to draw upon the insights of modern thought and address the modern reader. The nineteenth-century debate between Christianity and science was here transmuted into twentieth-century criticism of primitive Christian anthropology.

Matthews alerts us to the danger of shackling Christology in patristic chains. Faith must remain self-critical about the forms in which it is expressed. A Christology which has no response to scientific criticism of Jesus' person and ministry, his ethics and miracles, risks confining Jesus to a primitive worldview. The nineteenth-century *Lives of Jesus* movement reveals the opposite danger. Jesus

19. W. R. Matthews, *The Problem of Christ in the Twentieth Century: An Essay on the Incarnation*, The Maurice Lectures, 1949 (London: Oxford University Press, 1951), 12.

20. Matthews, *Problem of Christ*, lecture 2, "The Classical Theology."

21. Matthews, *Problem of Christ*, lecture 3, "Towards a Modern Christology."

there became a nineteenth-century figure with nineteenth-century values. As Albert Schweitzer warned: "There is no historical task which so reveals someone's true self as the writing of a life of Jesus." The quest to make Jesus relevant or intelligible risks rapid obsolescence and partiality. The Bultmann who critiqued the primitive inadequacy of the gospel account of Jesus, became the Bultmann later accused of subjectivity and scientism. This is not to say that science has not had and should not have an impact on Christology. Rather, that impact, because it is essentially fluid or transitory, offers no additional security or necessary support to the self-critical Christologian. "The impact of science" is simply part of the complexity of "the christological problem."

6. The Problem of Christology for the Christian Church

To this point, "the christological problem" has been explored in relation to theological method and epistemology, evangelism and exegesis, historical theology and dogmatic orthodoxy. Jesus has been "considered" in his sovereign humanity and mysterious majesty as "the author and finisher" of salvation. As claimed in section one, biography, theology, history, psychology, spirituality, philosophy, and sociology have converged. In the last section (in discussion of Harnack and Matthews), we glimpsed the tension found in Christology today between "the faith of the church" and the questions of the academy. Whether it be in the liberalism of Bultmann, the postmodernism of Don Cupitt, or the reductionism of Bishop Spong, classical Christian teaching today on the incarnation, virgin birth, miraculous ministry, resurrection, and return of Jesus Christ has been subjected to substantial reconstruction or wholesale rejection. Whatever we think of this, "the christological problem" remains an *ecclesiological* problem. For Jesus Christ is central to the faith, sacraments, and missionary endeavor of the church.

Recall, for a moment, that earlier quotation from E. L. Mascall (see above section two):

That the Christ whom we know today is the historic Christ is basic to our faith, but we do not depend for our acquaintance with Him on the research of historians and archaeologists. He is also the heavenly Christ, and as such is the object of our present experience, mediated through the sacramental life of the Church.

Mascall provides a healthy antidote to scholarly preoccupation with how much we do — or, more often, do *not* — know about the life of Jesus Christ. As an Anglo-Catholic, Mascall's perspective is unashamedly traditional, heavenly, and sacramental. This is consonant with the Christologies of 1 Corinthians, Ephesians, and Colossians. There, as in Mascall, the exalted Christ is the living, life-giving, grace-bestowing "Head" of the church and cosmic "Lord" over all. It is a perspective contemporary Christology would do well to remember. But Mascall also sees the church as (in some sense) an "extension" of the incarnation in its mission, ministry, and sacramental life. It embodies in its corporate sacramental worship and ordained ministerial life a living witness to the eternal sacrifice and priesthood of Christ. Both lines of christological reflection in Mascall ground theology in the dynamic life of the historic church and safeguard it against the vicissitudes of scholarly debate. Christology finds in ecclesiology a goad to critical thought and a guardian of traditional thought.

Mascall's perspective is neither unique nor quirky. Michael Ramsey's brief monograph *The Gospel and the Catholic Church* (1937), which did much to revitalize Anglican reflection on the church's faith, sacraments, ministry, and devotional life, explicitly rooted itself in the life, death, and resurrection of Jesus Christ. As he writes at the outset, "This book is written as a study of the Church, and its doctrine, and unity and structure, in terms of the Gospel of Christ crucified and risen."[22] Bonhoeffer's *Christ the Center* presents a similarly christocentric ecclesiology. There, as in Mascall, Christology shapes ecclesiology and is in turn shaped by it. If, to the Reformed Karl Barth, "Dogmatics must actually be Christology and only Christology"; to the liberal Anglican Ramsey and the dialectical

22. Arthur Michael Ramsey, *The Gospel and the Catholic Church* (London: Longmans, Green and Co., 1937), 5.

theologian Bonhoeffer, "*Ecclesiology* must actually be Christology and only Christology."

The problem of Christology for the Christian church today is, then, about reconciling difficult debates about "the Jesus of history" with ongoing personal and sacramental experience of "the Christ of faith." The eighteenth-century Enlightenment thrust this issue to the fore (in its fascination with history): postmodernism today keeps the issue alive (in its fascination with experience). From this last point two further points derive.

First, "the christological problem" today, as it pertains to ecclesiology, involves honoring popular appeals for an experiential Christian spirituality whilst regulating experience according to accredited Christian criteria. This is not easy; but it's *very* necessary. Without it "experience" is unrecognizably Christian and historic Christianity unfortunately lost. For the postmodern mind is famously suspicious of intellectual authorities and remarkably eclectic in its creative spiritualities. In the face of this, Christology cannot be restrictedly "rational" (denying experience a place in Christian theology) nor naively "experiential" (denying reason and "orthodoxy" a regulative role).

Secondly, the challenge of trying to honor Mascall's (and again Bonhoeffer's) sense of the heavenly Christ, who is sovereign over the church and present in its worship, lies in doing this without falling into either cosmic mysticism or socially insensitive religious imperialism (be it in tone, style, or content). The tradition which establishes strong connections between Christology and ecclesiology needs critical reexamination in today's relativist, multicultural world. This is not to say that Christians cannot and should not continue to celebrate Jesus Christ as "Lord over all" and "Head of the church," but that they do so in a new world, with new possibilities for provocation, offense, and misunderstanding.

The problem of Christology for the Christian church as we enter the third millennium is, then, considerable. It is made more problematic by the widespread spiritual hunger that craves a genuine experience and the rampant popular culture that is suspicious of classical Christian authority, terminology, and wrangling. The church is called in faith to "consider him" who is not only the "author" (in history) of its faith but also its "finisher" (in eternity). The church trusts to *this* Christ as active in and over *his* body, the church, *his* presence and power "the same yesterday, today and forever."

7. The Problem of Christology
for the Committed Disciple

The final slice of the christological steak is more personal. It asks about the problem of Christology for the committed disciple. What of the one who wants to understand, wants to think, wants to evangelize, wants to be faithful to the Scriptures and the faith of the church, wants to find an answer to the bothersome question regarding who Christ really is for us today, or, as Bonhoeffer asked in his lectures on Christology, "Where is Christ in the thought and life of church and society today?"[23]

Many of the problems faced intellectually and corporately by the whole Christian community are experienced individually and spiritually by each committed Christian. We wonder how much we know of him. We wrestle with understanding his divinity and humanity, and their relationship within him. We struggle with the sufficiency, authority, and integrity of the New Testament accounts concerning him. We look to the questions of history and take our gaze off his celebrated sovereignty. We consider his abject weakness and wonder about his uniqueness. We name him "Lord" but struggle to honor him as such. Many of the problems felt by the whole church are known in each individual part, in the heart and mind of each individual disciple.

Let me suggest five specific issues in the field of Christology that are felt with particular intensity at the individual level:

a. *The relationship between faithful discipleship and "the imitation of Christ"* — the issue being the propriety, the adequacy, and the invariability of a disciple of Jesus following not only Jesus' morality and spirituality but also his lifestyle and teaching.

23. Dietrich Bonhoeffer, *Christ the Center* (New York: Harper & Row, 1978), 59ff.

b. *The role of Jesus in the disciple's prayer.* Christology, to be a living, breathing, intellectual and spiritual discipline, cannot long talk about Jesus Christ as God-Man or mediator without considering his place in the church's prayer. At the individual level the issue is not only Jesus' mediation of prayer but his pattern for private prayer.

c. *The place of Jesus' humanity and atonement in the church's pastoral and healing ministry.* If Christology is to speak in living faith of *this* Jesus of the Gospels and not another, it can but speak in tones that convey this one's identification with those in sickness, pain, and sin. Such themes cannot be treated at arm's length. *This* historical individual *then* touches *this* historical individual *now.* I want to know what his life means for *me,* in relation to *my* sin, *my* pain, *my* sickness. If Christology is disconnected from pastoral theology it is disconnected from Jesus in the Gospels. To what, then, does it bear witness if not to *his* life, *his* message, *his* dynamic ministry?

d. *The power of this Jesus to atone for my sin, and carry my guilt.* I have not spoken much of the cross. Traditionally, Christology concerns the person *and* work of Jesus Christ. It seeks understanding of his atoning death, resurrection, heavenly exaltation, session, sympathetic intercession, and final return. One word on these: They can be considered with "detachment": "invested" Christology asks rather, for good and ill, what they mean personally. What does his death mean *for me?* Is he raised to new life *in me?* Do I trust that he reigns in heaven and prays *for me?* His life and work are, as Luther and Bonhoeffer stressed, *pro me* (for me). Luther warned on one occasion, "Many are lost because they cannot use the personal pronoun. It is *my* Lord and my God." He died *for me:* that is Christology come to life. "The christological problem" is an intensely *personal* one.

e. *"The christological problem" for the committed disciple concerns faith and hope in Jesus in the face of death.* Christology rightly asks, Is this crucified one who shared the world's pain and died the world's death there on the other side of *my* death? Has he "gone to prepare a place"[24] *for me?* This is the right place for this paper to end. For "the

24. John 14:3.

christological problem" must engage with the existential problems of human life and mortality. This is part of the amazing complexity of both Christ and Christology, part of the amazing truth and beauty to which *his* life and death bear singular witness.

The Necessity of a
Biblical Christology

RICHARD REID

The question that I have been asked to address is, "Why do we need to have a biblical Christology?" It is a very important question, but it depends, of course, on the assumption that we need to have a Christology at all. That issue is what this volume is seeking to address. The book's title poses the question: "Who do you say that I am?" It is the question that Jesus put explicitly to his disciples, and that he puts implicitly, by his words and actions, to all who encounter him. It is, in fact, the essential question for the church and, we believe, also for the whole world. Many answers have been given to that question. The disciples had already answered Jesus' earlier question concerning what others said about him. Then, as now, there were many different opinions about who Jesus was and what significance he had for the lives of those who encountered him. Peter, speaking for the other disciples, answered the question, according to the earliest of the Gospels, St. Mark's, "You are the Christ." In Matthew's version of the story the answer is longer, "You are the Christ, the Son of the living God."

How we answer the question is vitally important. The Scottish theologian D. M. Baillie said, "If we have not a sound Christology, we cannot have a sound theology either." That statement is certainly true, for how we understand Christ will radically affect how we understand God. The Anglican theologian and former Archbishop of Canterbury, William Temple, puts it this way, "The functions which He [Christ] discharges are functions of God. Now functions, that is actions and reactions, are all we know. If Jesus performs the acts of God, then Jesus Christ is God in the only sense in which any name can justifiably be attributed to any object."[1] Temple assumes that the biblical accounts of Jesus' actions and the interpretation given to them are reliable. I share that assumption. To make that assumption in faith leads to the conclusion that the classical Christology expressed in the doctrine of the incarnation, that Jesus Christ is "truly God and truly man," is valid. There are many today, as there have been in other generations, who wish to deny the truth of the incarnation. My conviction is that the doctrine of the incarnation is essential to the Christian faith. To deny it is to opt for a different religion. Another Anglican theologian, Bishop Charles Gore, writing in 1891, said, "I do not think it can be reasonably gainsaid that Christianity has meant historically, faith in the person of Jesus Christ, considered as very God incarnate, so much so that if this faith were gone, Christianity in its characteristic features would be gone also." (Sometimes writers in the Victorian period say things in ways that may be a trifle confusing to us. Perhaps I could paraphrase Bishop Gore this way: "No incarnation, no Christianity.")

To this point I have been talking about the necessity of a Christology, the necessity of responding to the question, "Who do you say that I am?" It is very important how we respond to that question. But these are not the exact issues that I was asked to address. Yet these issues are necessary as a basis for a discussion of the "Necessity of a Biblical Christology," and it is to that question that we must now turn.

For us as Anglicans there is a formal answer to this question. Christology is, as I have said, an important, indeed a central, Christian doctrine. Historically Anglicanism has always held that all doctrine must be rooted and grounded in Scripture. That is part of our Reformation heritage, although it is true that other communions,

1. William Temple, *Christus Veritas* (London: Macmillan, 1925), 113.

even those that do not share in the Reformation tradition, also hold that Scripture is vitally important for doctrine. Our tradition is very clear. The oath which every person being ordained as Bishop, Priest, or Deacon, takes says: "I . . . solemnly declare that I do believe the Holy Scriptures of the Old and New Testaments to be the Word of God, and to contain all things necessary to salvation. . . ." If Christology is as important as I have indicated, then a proper Christology must, of necessity, be based on the Holy Scriptures. Article VI of the Articles of Religion puts the matter even more clearly. "Holy Scripture containeth all things necessary to salvation: so that whatsoever is not read therein nor may be proved thereby, is not to be required of any man, that it should be believed as an article of the Faith, or be thought requisite or necessary to salvation." I know that not everyone in the Episcopal Church regards the Thirty-nine Articles as having any real authority. I am quite willing to acknowledge their authority, and, especially on the point we are discussing, they seem to me to express the mind of Anglicanism.

If I may digress for just a moment, it is interesting to note how much things have changed since the Articles were written. The issue at the time of the Reformation, as the article I just quoted makes clear, was to prevent people from being required to believe too much. All the medieval teachings about purgatory, and indulgences, and works of supererogation, for example, were not based on Scripture and could not therefore be required. In our day the problem seems to be the other way around. We need to base our doctrine and Christology on the Scriptures lest we believe too little. Liberal Christianity in the nineteenth century turned Jesus simply into a profound teacher and the preeminent role model. Some people today seem to be suggesting that he can be seen in a similar fashion, though with perhaps more of a countercultural element in his lifestyle.

I have, then, given the formal answer to the question of the necessity of a biblical Christology. But since most of us do not like to take authoritative statements simply at face value without seeing why they were made, I wish to explore the reasons why it is important to have a *biblical* Christology. The authoritative statements are not simply arbitrary dicta handed down from the past. They are the distillation of the wisdom of the church, and they are based on an understanding of the nature of the Christian revelation and the relationship of the Bible to that revelation. In the remainder of this lecture I intend to explore with you the essential contribution that the Bible makes to our understanding of Christology. I shall attempt to do this by discussing three closely related topics. First, a biblical Christology is necessary because the Bible provides the *context* for all our christological statements. Second, the Bible gives us the *content* for our Christology. Third, the Bible makes it possible to affirm the *continuity* between our christological affirmations and the words and deeds of Jesus himself.

The Context of Christology

To talk about Christ or Christology at all is at once to put our discussion into the context of the biblical story and in particular of the Old Testament. We have become so accustomed to using the words Jesus Christ that we may assume that both words are really part of his name. But, in fact, the name by which he was known was simply Jesus, or sometimes to distinguish him from others who had the same name, Jesus of Nazareth. The word "Christ" was originally not a name, but a title. The proper form was really Jesus, the Christ. Christ is the Greek form of the Hebrew word, "messiah," which means "anointed." Jesus was the "anointed one," the Messiah. To use that title for Jesus is, at once, to place him in the context of the Old Testament. In Israel kings, priests, and sometimes prophets were anointed. They were people who had a special role in the life of the people of God, and the sacrament of that role was their anointing. It was the "outward and visible sign" of God's blessing and empowerment for the task they were called to do. In the Book of Isaiah, even a pagan king is called a messiah. In chapter 45 the prophet we know as Second Isaiah says, "Thus says the Lord to his anointed, to Cyrus, whose right hand I have grasped, to subdue nations before him and ungird the loins of kings, to open doors before him that gates may not be closed. 'I will go before you and level the mountains, I will break in pieces the doors of bronze and cut asunder the bars of iron.'" Cyrus was the Persian king who had conquered the Babylonians and set free the people of Israel who had been living in exile. Cyrus had his part to play in the story of the people of God. He was at that moment "God's Messiah."

Isaiah goes on to give more of what God said to Cyrus. "I will give you the treasures of darkness, and the hoards in secret places that you may know that it is I, the Lord, who call you by your name. For the sake of my servant Jacob, and Israel my chosen, I call you by your name, I surname you, though you do not know me. I am the Lord, and there is no other, beside me there is no God; I gird you though you do not know me, that men may know, from the rising of the sun and from the west, that there is none beside me; I am the Lord, and there is no other." Cyrus, though he does not really understand what is happening, is carrying out the purposes of God, of the only God there is. And he is doing it for the sake of God's people — for Israel and ultimately for the whole world. That is what a "messiah" does. To call Jesus "the Messiah" is to place him in the context of the story of God's people — a story which begins with Abraham and comes down through Isaac and Jacob, and Moses, and Saul and David and Solomon and all the prophets. It is an unfinished story in the Old Testament. By Jesus' time the people were hoping and longing for a fulfillment, for rescue from the oppression of the Romans. They were hoping for a messiah who would set them free, so that they might once again be God's people in the Holy Land which God had given them. There were many different forms of that hope and expectation. Some thought it would come through a revolt led by a new king in the tradition of David. Others hoped for a new Moses who would renew the people's commitment to the Law. Others hoped that Elijah, the first of the prophets, would come back and restore the fortunes of the people. Whatever form it took the hope was always that God would act to fulfill his promises and to put right what had gone wrong.

The claim of the New Testament is that God has now done just that. He has acted in Christ. He has acted decisively and finally. The opening verses of the Epistle to the Hebrews put the point very clearly. "In many and various ways God spoke of old to our fathers by the prophets; but in these last days he has spoken to us by a Son, whom he appointed the heir of all things. . . ." In the past God spoke, that is, God revealed himself by what he did and said, in a variety of ways. He spoke by the prophets who, for Hebrews, included a much wider group than we call prophets. Moses, for example, was a prophet. But now, in these last days, he has spoken to us by a Son. The phrase "in these last days" is a bit misleading. It can mean in English, "recently." If I say to you — "In these last days we have had a lot of rain" — I mean to convey the fact that it has rained often in the last week or two. But the Greek that Hebrews is using does not mean that. It means "at the end of these days," at the end of the era of history in which his readers had all been living. The language is what theologians call "eschatological." Hebrews is claiming that the Son stands at the decisive turning point in history. He inaugurates "the new age," the time when Israel's hopes and expectations will be fulfilled. The Son is the heir of all things — he inherits all that the Old Testament promised. I said earlier that the story of the Old Testament is an unfinished story. Hebrews declares that now the final chapter in that story has come. And Hebrews is not alone in saying that. Throughout the New Testament Jesus is presented as the one who brings to fulfillment all that God had promised in the Old Testament. To take just a couple of examples: he is the new Moses who from the mountain gives a new interpretation of the Law which God sets before his people. He is the new David who rides through the cheering crowds into the capital city of Jerusalem. Like the great prophets of old, Elijah and Elisha, he performs miracles. What I am saying is that it is impossible to understand the ministry of Jesus as it is presented in the New Testament apart from the story of the Old Testament. I think that almost everyone who reads the New Testament carefully would agree that to understand it you have to refer back to the Old Testament.

I now wish to discuss the implications of the fact that Jesus must be understood in the context of the Old Testament. The first and most important point to be made is that the God of the Old Testament is also the God of the New Testament. That point may seem so obvious that it is unnecessary for me to say it. But it has been denied in the course of Christian history. The first time was very early on. In the second century, a man in Rome, named Marcion, declared that the God described in the Old Testament, the God who created the world and called Israel, was a different God from the God and Father of Jesus. The God of the Old Testament was, he declared, a lesser god, a god of wrath, a vindictive god, a god of law quite unlike the God of love revealed in the New Testament. He decided that the church should no longer read the Old Testament at all. He also decided that the only scriptures to be used were the Gospel of Luke and the letters of Paul, somewhat edited to remove as many references to the Old Testament as possible.[2] The church declared Marcion's views heretical. In spite of that fact, however, his views have continued. I have heard sermons actually saying that the God of the Old Testament is to be distinguished from the God of the New Testament in a way more or less like that of Marcion.

The Old Testament is the story of Israel. It is a wonderful story, a very human story, filled with interesting characters and events. It is easy to be caught up in the story of the struggles of Moses with the people in the wilderness. or the account of Joshua's conquest of the Holy Land. The struggles of a young nation, under the leadership of people like Deborah and Gideon, to protect itself from enemies that would destroy it make interesting reading. The development of kingship under Saul and then David and Solomon contains valuable insights into the political process. But, while all of this is very interesting, the central character in the story — of the Old Testament — is always God. God is the chief actor in all that happens, and the story develops the way that it does because God's purpose is being worked out. The Bible, both Old and New Testaments, is first and foremost a book about God.

We have already seen a glimpse of what I am saying in the passage I quoted from Isaiah about Cyrus. God acts through Cyrus to accomplish his purposes for Israel and the world, even though Cyrus does not acknowledge that fact. And Isaiah makes very clear who this God is. He is the Lord, the Holy One who is above all. He is sovereign. He will allow no competition. The God who is revealed in the biblical story is a God who demands obedience. That is a very

---

2. We actually owe Marcion a debt because he forced the church to think about what should be included in the New Testament.

important point. For to say that our understanding of who Christ is must be in the context of the Bible means that we must understand what the basic human problem is. If Christ is the fulfillment of the messianic hopes of the Old Testament, if he comes as a savior, then we need to know from what we are being saved. The biblical analysis of the human problem is that we are sinners. We disobey God.

It may seem unnecessary to say that sin is the basic human problem. Someone once said that the only Christian doctrine that is empirically verifiable is the doctrine of original sin. All you have to do is read the daily newspaper. There are certainly plenty of illustrations of evil and malicious behavior, but I am not really sure that those facts confirm what we mean by sin. Sin in the biblical understanding is a kind of power that has us in its grip. It is the desire we all have to have life on our terms rather than God's. We are unwilling to let God be God. The story that illustrates what I am saying is, of course, the story of Adam and Eve. All I need to do is remind you that the point of the story is that Adam and Eve are tempted to eat the fruit of the tree of the knowledge of good and evil because, if they do so, the devil says, they will be like God. The point of that story is not to tell about a particular event but to illustrate what is true of all people. We all want to be in control. We want to be like God or at least we want to choose the gods that we will have. John Calvin said that the human heart is an idol factory. We make idols out of money or power, or social position, or sex, or food, or national pride, or any of a few thousand other things. The heart of the matter is that we want to be like God. Just one simple illustration: God has the power to create reality by his word. When God said "Let there be light," there was light. When we try to create reality by our word, we end up telling a lie. We cannot change reality just by saying that something is or is not so and yet we often try to do so, as recent events in the United States have shown. A biblical Christology must take into account that the basic human problem is sin.

Lest you think that it is not necessary to say this let me remind you that many people advocate other definitions of the basic human problem. Lack of education, for example. Some people argue that, if only we could insure that everyone was properly educated all human problems would be solved. I hope I will not be misunderstood here. I am definitely in favor of education. I have spent virtually my whole life as either a student or a teacher. But education, vital though it is, does not deal with the basic problem. If you educate a sinner, what you get is an educated sinner. Others claim that the basic human problem is corrupt institutions or systems. They never seem to explain how institutions or economic and political systems become corrupted in the first place.

Let me give you one further illustration. It is the story of Abraham. Abraham is the founder of the people of Israel. He is a man of faith. The Bible describes Abraham as "the friend of God," and both the Old and the New Testaments cite him as a preeminent example of a person of faith. Yet even Abraham illustrates what I have been saying. When God comes to Abraham and tells him that he and Sarah are to have a son, an heir, Abraham has a moment of doubt. He is one hundred years old and Sarah is ninety. The birth of a son to them seems impossible. Yet God is saying that the future of the holy people, the fulfillment of the promise that Abraham will be "the father of many nations," depends on the birth of this son. But Abraham already has a son. His name is Ishmael. He is the son of Abraham and Sarah's maid, Hagar, since Sarah up to this point had been unable to conceive a child. And so Abraham tries to bargain with God.[3] Abraham says to God, "Let Ishmael live in thy sight." In effect Abraham is saying to God, "Look, God, you are asking something that is really impossible. I want the promise to be fulfilled, but let's do it my way. Why won't Ishmael do?" But this time Abraham doesn't win in the bargaining. For to do so would be to compromise the sovereignty of God. Ishmael was born out of Abraham's normal desire to have a son and heir, a desire that was even more important in his time than in ours, for having an heir was the assurance of immortality, of the continuance of the family with all that that meant. But we are not talking here about the fulfillment of human desires — we are not in control. Not even God's friend, Abraham. God will be God. He will see to it that his promises are fulfilled in his own *way*. And so, impossible though it seemed, Abraham and Sarah do have a son named Isaac.

3. Abraham tried on another occasion to bargain with God, and that time he was successful.

The importance of the Bible as the context of our Christology is that it provides us with the understanding of the sovereignty of God and helps us to see that the basic human problem from which we need salvation is the problem of sin. It also does two more very important things. First, it gives us an understanding of the nature of the sovereign God. The God who reveals himself in the Old Testament story is a God of mercy and compassion as well as a God of righteousness and truth. The first two of those words are probably clear to everyone. God is merciful and compassionate. He forgives the sins of Israel. The story of Israel includes countless occasions on which God's people refused to obey him — times when they, as the Bible puts it, "went after other gods." The golden calf in the wilderness comes quickly to mind. There were also many others. After they came into the promised land they were always trying to hedge their bets by setting up altars to and worshipping the local gods of the land, the baals, as they were called. It was the theological version of "when in Rome, do as the Romans do." The people in Palestine had been worshipping these gods for a long time. It would be safer not to rock the boat. But the Lord, the God of Abraham and Isaac and Jacob, was very clear that Israel was to have no other gods. Israel was punished for her disobedience, as she had been at the time of the golden calf. But God forgave. Even after the exile God forgave his people and brought them back. God is a God of mercy and compassion.

He is also a God of righteousness and truth. Instead of the word "righteousness," the word "justice" is also sometimes used. And that does give part of the meaning. God is a God of justice. He cares that his creation and his people be treated fairly. That issue, too, must be part of our Christology. But righteousness also has a broader meaning. It is a more active quality. It means that God intends to put things right — to bring his world into a right relationship with himself. And truth — truth also has a little different meaning from what we may think. The Hebrew word used for truth is related to a very familiar word, the word *amen*. When we say *amen* after a prayer we are confirming what has been said. The root behind the Hebrew word means "to be firm, dependable, reliable." God is a God of truth for he is dependable. He can be relied on to keep his promises, to do what he says he will do. As you hear and read the

Psalms, notice how often these words, mercy, compassion, righteousness, and truth, occur. I cite just one example because it is important for Christology. Psalm 85 is a prayer for deliverance — a prayer that God will act to save his people. It asks God to "show mercy" and "grant salvation." And then it assures the people that God's salvation is near. And it gives this lovely poetic description of what that time will be like. "Mercy and truth have met together; righteousness and peace have kissed each other." That is a description of the messianic age. In the New Testament the Epistle to the Hebrews recognizes this and relates it closely to Jesus. Hebrews sees a type, a foreshadowing of the Christ in a rather obscure figure from the Old Testament, a royal priest named Melchizedek. Melchizedek, Hebrews says, resembles the Son of God. And part of the reason is his title and his name. He is the King of Salem, which means peace, and his name means "the king of righteousness." In Melchizedek, as a forerunner of Christ, and now in the fullness of time in Christ himself, "righteousness and peace have kissed each other." The promise is fulfilled.

The second thing that a biblical Christology preserves for us is the universal nature of God's plan. As the passage from Isaiah reminds us, God called Israel to be his people. But God is the creator of the whole world. God cares for all people. The purpose of Israel is to be a "light to the nations" to bear witness to God so that all may know him. The salvation brought by Christ is the fulfillment of that promise. A biblical Christology describes a Christ who comes to save the world — to call all people to the knowledge and love of God. He comes to restore and put right what went wrong back in the Garden of Eden. He renews the whole created order. That is the way the Bible ends. There is a new creation. The vision of the final chapters of the Book of Revelation is of a great city, a city which has in it the tree of life, and into which all the nations of the world will come.

The Content of Christology

Up to this point I have been discussing the *context* of Christology. I have focused on the Old Testament as the major factor in the context of Christology and on the identity of the God who acts in both the Old and New Testament stories. I must turn now to my second topic, the *content* of a biblical Christology. I can treat this subject much more briefly because another chapter on the "Biblical Formation of a Doctrine of Christ" will deal with the subject at more length. But there are three points that are central to my concern for the necessity of a biblical Christology.

The first one is that Christology concerns the person named Jesus. Jesus is a real person who lived at a particular time and in a particular place, as do all human beings. The Swiss New Testament scholar Oscar Cullmann puts the point very clearly. In his book *The Christology of the New Testament,* he says, "All Christology is founded upon the life of Jesus."[4] That may seem to be an obvious statement, but it is one that we need to keep in mind. Christianity is not about some abstract ideas — it is about a person named Jesus and the significance he has for our lives and for the world. The Czech scholar Petr Pokorny states the issue very clearly: "The historicity with which Christology has to reckon depends not only on the changing historical milieu of the Church but above all on the incarnation of God, which the oldest Christian statements directly or indirectly attest. This is how the Christian faith differs from general religious tendencies. The orientation of faith thus depends on the remembrance of Jesus, the norm of faith is tied to a particular time and is mediated through tradition. Otherwise there would be no way of checking on religious discourse, it could not be distinguished from fantasy."[5] Our faith is tied to a particular historical event — the life of Jesus. The only reliable access we have to that life is through the Bible. The Gospels and some references in the rest of the New Testament are really the only sources we have for what Jesus did and said.[6] We are, for all practical purposes, dependent primarily on the

4. Oscar Cullmann, *The Christology of the New Testament* (Philadelphia: Westminster Press, 1963), 317.

5. Petr Pokorny, *The Genesis of Christology* (Edinburgh: T & T Clark, 1987), 11.

6. There are a few other books, apocryphal gospels, and a collection of sayings attributed to Jesus in a book called the Gospel of Thomas. The latter may contain some echoes of Jesus' teaching but it is later than the Gospels and heavily influenced by a system of thought quite different from the Bible.

Gospels, and to a lesser extent, on the other New Testament books for what we know about Jesus. If Cullmann and Pokorny are right, and I believe that they are, then our Christology must be based on the New Testament.

The second thing that needs to be said is that the Gospels provide us with a reliable picture of Jesus. They portray Jesus as a man with a deep relationship to God, a man of prayer, a man with a sense of mission and with a calling to preach and teach. He is not afraid to challenge some of the accepted ideas of his day, and he invites those who hear him to leave their old ways and turn and follow him. He is a man of love and compassion. He reaches out to the outcasts of society. He includes in his followers tax collectors and prostitutes, and even speaks kindly of the hated Samaritans. He forgives the woman taken in adultery and tells her to sin no more. He instructs his disciples to forgive others not just seven times but seventy times seven. (In a world that did not usually think in millions not to mention billions, that really means an unlimited number of times.) He shows concern for those in his world who were especially vulnerable, the poor, children, widows, and those with handicaps. He teaches an ethic of justice, and yet one of mercy and love. Our Christology must take into account the portrayal of Jesus as a man, a very particular kind of man, and our source for understanding that man is clearly the Bible.

But the Gospels also make clear that there is more that needs to be said about Jesus. He speaks and acts in very special ways. He teaches, not like the scribes and Pharisees, but with authority. In the Sermon on the Mount he speaks not as the teachers of Israel did or even like the prophets who said "Thus saith the Lord." Jesus said, "You have heard that it was said to the men of old . . . but I say unto you." He spoke in his own name, and people wondered at his authority. He fulfilled the prophecies of the Old Testament, but not always as the people expected him to do. I noted earlier that he was a new David, who rode into Jerusalem. But he came not as a conqueror or as a political leader. He came in peace riding on an ass, and he did not even attempt to throw the Romans out of the city. Indeed he accepted their rule and ordered that their taxes should be paid. He made the eschatological proclamation: "The time is fulfilled, and the kingdom of God is at hand, repent and believe in the gospel." He acted out the signs of the time of fulfillment. He healed the sick and raised the dead, and proclaimed good news to the poor. He called twelve disciples, a sign of the reconstituting of the people of God, the twelve tribes of Israel. What I am saying goes back to the quotation I read from Archbishop Temple. The Gospels portray Jesus as carrying out the functions of God. He speaks and acts like no one else. And it is not just the Gospels. Klaas Runia, referring to the remarkable unity in the New Testament, once said, "All writers, one way or another, put Jesus on the side of God." A biblical Christology requires that we take into account this fact as well as the reality of Jesus' humanity. The New Testament portrays him as a man, but as a man who acts in ways that are appropriate only to God.

The third thing that needs to be said in this section on the *content* of a biblical Christology is the most important. Almost all the books of the New Testament refer to it and it is always at the heart of the whole story. I am referring, of course, to Jesus' death and resurrection. His death at the hands of the Romans was, as Paul puts it in 1 Corinthians, a stumbling block to the Jews. The Messiah was not supposed to be defeated but to triumph. Paul goes on to say, "The word of the cross is folly to those who are perishing but to us who are being saved it is the power of God." The cross looks like weakness, but Paul assures us that it is "the power of God." The reason he can say that is that Paul was aware of what I talked about earlier — the nature of the human problem. We need to be free — free from the power of sin. The earliest summary of the gospel that we have comes in Paul's first letter to the Corinthians. He reminds the church in Corinth of the gospel which he first preached to them, a gospel that he himself had received. He says, "I delivered to you as of first importance what I also received, that Christ died for our sins in accordance with the scriptures." That is at the heart of gospel message. Everything else that the Bible says about Jesus is important, but this is the most important. He died for our sins. Please notice that Paul says that he died *for* our sins, and not because of them (though that is true also). It was not just that we human sinners put Jesus to death to get him out of our way. He died for our sins. He died to do something about the fundamental human problem. All the doctrines of the atonement are attempts to explain what that little word *for* meant. But clearly one thing it means for us is that our Christology must recognize that in some way Christ's death has dealt with the basic human problem of sin.

One form of biblical Christology that does that is the one that we find in several places in the New Testament, but especially in Paul's Letter to the Philippians, chapter 2. It is the passage that we hear in the Liturgy on Palm Sunday. I will not quote it all because I hope that it is familiar and because I want to deal with only one part. It begins, "Have this mind among yourselves which you have in Christ Jesus, who though he was in the form of God did not count equality with God a thing to be grasped, but emptied himself. . . . he humbled himself and became obedient unto death, even death on a cross." That passage, I believe, has its roots in the story of Adam. It presents Jesus as the new Adam. Unlike the old Adam Jesus does not wish to cling on to equality with God. He does not seek to be in control. He becomes obedient even unto death, even to the excruciating and humiliating death on a cross. And by doing that he reverses what Adam did.

Let me try to make as clear as I can just what I mean. Sin always presents itself to us as an attractive option. The devil, so to speak, says, "If you will obey me you will have a better life." Most of the time the temptation may be relatively minor. Eat this extra piece of chocolate cake (you can tell the kind of temptation I am easily vulnerable to) — eat this piece of cake because you will enjoy it — it will make your life a little better, and, anyway, you deserve a little reward for all that you have had to put up with. Sometimes the temptation is about a much more serious matter. But the basics are the same. The threat which the devil makes is that, if you do not obey him, your life will be diminished. And the final threat of the devil is "Obey me or I will kill you." Those of you who remember the Eichmann trial will recall that that was his defense. He either obeyed Hitler or Hitler would have him executed. He either killed the Jews or died himself. Adam was promised life if he ate the apple — and not just life, but he would be like God. To refuse that temptation could only be compared to death. Jesus faced that situation in Gethsemane. He knew that if he continued his mission and did not slip away, he would be killed. He prayed that the cup, the cup of suffering, might be taken away. But he ended the prayer, "Not my will but thine be done." Whereas Adam was disobedient to God, Jesus lived out his vocation of obedience. The devil threatened to kill him if he did not sin, and Jesus said, in effect, all right kill me. He was obedient even to death, and thereby he reversed what Adam had done. He broke the power of sin, and his death was for us, he died for our sins. There are other images used for the meaning of Christ's death: sacrifice, justification, reconciliation, for example. It is always clear that in each of them God is acting to put right what has gone wrong, and that his sending of Christ to die for our sins is the supreme act of God's love. That is the heart of the gospel, and it must be at the heart of any biblical Christology.

The New Testament is clear that at the center of its message is the proclamation that Christ died for our sins, for the sins of the world. It is, of course, equally clear that God raised him from the dead. The death of Christ is only "gospel," good news, because of the resurrection. Paul is very clear about this. His summary of his preaching to the church in Corinth to which I referred earlier does not end with the statement that "Christ died for our sins." It goes on to say "He was raised on the third day in accordance with the scriptures, and that he appeared to Cephas (Peter), and then to the twelve." He continues with accounts of the risen Christ's other appearances. Please note that Paul says that Christ "was raised," the passive voice. The clear meaning is that God raised him. Only God can raise the dead. The resurrection was the act of God that makes clear the meaning of Jesus' death. It too was part of God's plan. It was the means of dealing with the fundamental problem of human beings and of the whole creation. It was the beginning of the final chapter in God's plan of salvation. Paul makes this view clear later on in the same chapter of 1 Corinthians. Some people in Corinth were denying the resurrection. Paul stresses both its truth and its importance. And then he says, "If Christ has not been raised, your faith is futile, and you are still in your sins." Notice how he puts this. He does not say that if Christ has not been raised, you have no hope of eternal life. He says that if Christ has not been raised you are still in your sins. The cross does not deal with the basic human problem of sin if Christ has not been raised. His death does not have its essential gospel meaning. It would be instead just another tragic death in a world that has seen lots of such deaths. But when God acts to raise Jesus, he confirms that his death too was part of God's plan, God's plan to deal with sin and to restore the whole creation. It is impossible to separate Jesus' death from the resurrection. That too is part of a biblical Christology.

The Continuity of Biblical Christology

We come now to the third and final topic, the continuity of biblical Christology. I have been discussing the context for Christology in the Bible, and have stressed that the Bible presents Jesus as the fulfillment of the Old Testament promises. I have also described, more briefly, how the New Testament presents Jesus. I wish now in this final section to make clear that there is continuity between the interpretation given of Jesus in the New Testament and the classical Christian understanding of Jesus as "truly God and truly man" to which I have already referred. I wish also to show that there is continuity between the affirmations of the New Testament and Jesus' own understanding of his mission.

The reason for doing this is, of course, that this continuity is important, and that it has been challenged. Some scholars have argued that there is a very wide gap between what the very earliest followers of Jesus believed about him, even after the resurrection, and the Christology expressed in the writings of Paul and John for example. Other scholars, notably the Jesus Seminar, have argued that most of the sayings of Jesus do not really go back to him, but are formulations of the later church and reflect ideas quite different from those of Jesus himself. They claim, for example, that Jesus did not proclaim that the kingdom of God was near.

Charles Moule deals with the issue of continuity in his book, *The Origin of Christology*. He makes a careful distinction between "development" and "evolution." He defines the distinction this way: ". . . if, in my analogy, 'evolution' means the genesis of successive new species by mutations and natural selection along the way, 'development', by contrast, will mean something more like the growth, from immaturity to maturity of a single specimen within itself."[7] Professor Moule is using an analogy from the natural world. The application he makes to Christology is that the changes that have taken place in the way the New Testament understands who Jesus is, and what significance he has, are developmental. The changes are not so drastic as to suggest something entirely new. Instead Moule argues, and with substantial evidence to prove his point, that it is possible "to explain all the various estimates of Jesus reflected in the New Testament as, in essence, only attempts to describe what was already there from the beginning. They are not successive additions of something new, but only the drawing out and articulating of what is there."

To illustrate what Moule means, let me cite an example. The prologue of the Gospel of John expresses its Christology in these words: "In the beginning was the Word, and the Word was with God, and the Word was God. And the word became flesh and dwelt among us full of grace and truth; we have beheld his glory, glory as of the only Son from the Father." (These words from John are the basis of the classical Christology and of the confession that Christians make when we affirm the Creed.) There can be no doubt that those words represent a development. The disciples, as they traveled with Jesus around Galilee, did not use those words. But John's Christology is not an "evolution" — a new thing. All of the Gospels present Jesus as one who taught with authority. He forgave sins. He healed the sick, and even raised the dead. He proclaimed the coming of the Kingdom. In all the Gospels, as Archbishop Temple pointed out, Jesus carried out the functions of God. St. Paul, too, presents Jesus as more than just a man. He calls him "the Lord." He frequently uses expressions like "Grace to you and peace from God our Father and the Lord Jesus Christ" in which Christ is very closely identified with God, in this case as sharing with the Father in being the source of the divine gift of grace.

Up to this point, I have been arguing only that there is continuity in the way that the various New Testament authors present

---

7. Charles Moule, *The Origin of Christology* (Cambridge: Cambridge University Press, 1977), 2.

their answer to Jesus' question, "Who do you say that I am?" That fact is important. The earliest evidence we have supports the argument that the Christology of the church, the incarnation, which as Bishop Gore reminded us is an essential mark of our faith — that Christology is in continuity with the Christology of the authors of the New Testament. Moule extends the argument one step further.

All the books of the New Testament were written after the resurrection. They, of course, contain memories of events before Jesus' death and resurrection. But they were all written down after the resurrection. There can be no doubt that the powerful experience of the death and resurrection of Christ has shaped the way in which the New Testament writers present their story. But even when we discern differences in the way the authors present Jesus, it is clear that there is continuity among them — development but not evolution. But what about Jesus himself? How did he understand his mission and ministry?

This is a very big question. I can only sketch out an answer to it. It is clear that Jesus understood that he had a very special relation to God. His prayers, including his special way of addressing God as Abba, *Father,* demonstrate that. His sense of mission and his willingness to continue it, even in the knowledge that he was taking a great risk, also point in that direction. His calling of the twelve, which I take to be firmly grounded in fact, indicates that he saw himself as having a role in defining a new covenant community. His welcoming of sinners and other unacceptable people and his eating with them also points to a redefinition of the covenant community. His use of the term "Son of Man," a term which in the Book of Daniel is used as a symbol for the faithful people of God, is another pointer to his self-understanding. There is a long scholarly debate about this term. One thing is clear. In the Gospels only Jesus himself uses the term. Raymond Brown, whose recent death has deprived us of one of the great New Testament scholars of this century, says that this title was "remembered to have come from Jesus in a very affirmative manner."[8] He goes on to consider Mark 14:61-62. The High

---

8. Raymond Brown, *An Introduction to New Testament Christology* (London: Geoffrey Chapman/Mowbray, 1994), 99.

Priest asks Jesus the question, "Are you the Christ, the Son of the Blessed [that is, God]?" Jesus replies, "I am; and you will see the Son of Man sitting at the right hand of Power, and coming with the clouds of heaven." Brown says that in these words we may be close to the mindset and style of Jesus himself. That is, that as Jesus claims his role as God's agent in a moment when his life was at stake, he asserts that God will vindicate him and will bring in his kingdom.

Reginald Fuller also believes that Jesus understood himself as the "eschatological prophet" — that is, as the one who comes to speak for God and to declare the coming of the kingdom. He also believes that Jesus understood his death to be a significant factor in his role. He cites, in support of this view, two passages which preserve clear and accurate memories of what Jesus said.[9] The first is Luke 13:32-33. The Pharisees come and tell Jesus that Herod is seeking to kill him. Jesus replies, "Go and tell that fox, 'Behold I cast out demons and perform cures today and tomorrow, and the third day I finish my course. Nevertheless, I must go on my way today and tomorrow and the day following; for it cannot be that a prophet should perish away from Jerusalem." Jesus understands his exorcisms and healings as the signs *of* the kingdom, but he also understands that his prophetic role involves his death. The second passage is from the account of the Last Supper in Mark 14:25: "Truly, I say to you, I shall not drink again of the fruit of the vine until that day when I drink it new in the kingdom of God." In this passage Jesus distinguishes between himself and his disciples. He also relates his death closely to his proclamation of the kingdom. Fuller comments, "Here Jesus brings his death into direct association with the eschatological message of the kingdom of God which he had proclaimed throughout his ministry."

The importance of all this is that there is continuity between the message of Jesus and his own understanding of his ministry and mission, and even of his death. I referred earlier to the words of Pokorny. He said that our Christology "depends on the remem-

---

9. Reginald Fuller, *The Foundations of New Testament Christology* (New York: Scribner, 1965), 106f.

brance of Jesus." Our remembrance of Jesus in turn depends on the New Testament. A biblical Christology will keep that remembrance before us.

Conclusion

A biblical Christology is necessary because of the nature of the Christian faith. That faith is not based on an idea or an ideology. We are not talking about a "Christ principle." We are talking about a revelation from God which comes in and through real historical events. Jesus was a real man who lived in the real world. That means that he lived at a particular time and in a particular place. The Bible provides the only real access we have to that person. It provides us with information about him. It also interprets that information and helps us to understand its significance. The Bible also provides the context in which to understand Jesus. While there has been, and presumably will continue to be, development in Christology, any Christology which is not rooted in the Bible — which does not take into account the context, and the content, and the continuity which the Bible provides, will always be inadequate, or worse, just plain wrong. It may even turn Christianity into a different religion altogether.

The Biblical Formation
of a Doctrine of Christ

N. T. WRIGHT

The topic of this book could hardly be more central to the church's mission, work, and life today. Indeed, I have reflected recently that if our leaders spent more time studying and teaching biblical Christology a good many of the other things we worry about would be seen in their proper light. It has far too often been assumed that church leaders are above the nitty-gritty of biblical and theological study; that they have done all that before they come to office, and now simply have to work out the "implications." I believe, to the contrary, that each generation has to wrestle afresh with Christology, not least its biblical foundations, if it is to be truly the church at all. I do not mean that we should engage in abstract dogmatics to the detriment of our engagement with the world, but that we should discover more and more of who Jesus was and is precisely in order to be equipped to engage with the world that he came to save.

These preliminary reflections drive me to my own topic: the biblical formation of a doctrine of Christ. The word "Christ" in the title is to be understood in the broader, more common sense associated with the word "Christology": that is, that a "doctrine of Christ" is a way of saying something about Jesus and God in the same breath and with the same referent. Before we launch into that huge inquiry, I want to put down a warning mark for all those who find themselves tempted to use the word "Christ" in this sense without reflecting on its more nuanced biblical meaning. Precisely if we are to establish a *biblical* doctrine of Christ, we must be sure we know how the Bible itself uses the word.

The word "Christ" is of course the English version of the Greek *Christos,* which in turn stands for the Hebrew or Aramaic *Mashiach* or *Moshiach, Messiah.* The word means "the anointed one," and, though prophets and priests were also anointed, there is no real doubt that the word in the time of Jesus referred principally, if not univocally, to the anointed King. That is, specifically the King that some Jews at least hoped would come to liberate Israel from pagan oppression and set up YHWH's kingdom of justice and peace. With this word and this meaning, we are projected back into the turbulent world of first-century Judaism. There was in that time all sorts of would-be Messiahs, each one taking a different line; and all sorts of actual royal figures, notably the house of Herod, who likewise gave color to the idea of the Lord's anointed. There were Simon and Athronges, Judas the Galilean and his sons and grandsons, Menachem and Eleazar, Simon bar-Giora and Simeon ben-Kosiba, also known as bar-Kochba. The fact that most clergy, and most laity, have never heard of any of these characters is a sad measure of the way in which we have talked about Jesus of Nazareth without paying attention to his Jewish context. If anybody in the first century thought Jesus was God's Messiah, these were the people with whom they were inviting comparison.

I believe it is certain, historically, that Jesus believed himself to be the Messiah; but I believe it is also certain that he radically redefined that role around his own dramatically different sense of vocation. If Jesus was the Messiah, he was quite unlike what most if not all of his contemporaries — including John the Baptist and the Twelve — were expecting in such a figure. But the point I particularly wish to make at this preliminary stage is a different one. As far as we can tell, none of the other would-be Messiahs in the first century thought for a moment that they were in any sense "divine"; nor did their followers predicate any such thing of them. Since my task is to talk about the biblical basis of the Christian belief in the divinity of Jesus, the subject that is commonly called "Christology," I feel it incumbent on me to make this disclaimer. It is deeply misleading when we read the word "Christ," in the New Testament and particularly in the Gospels, as though the word itself meant "the divine one." As I shall show, the New Testament writers believed that Jesus, the Messiah, the Christ, was indeed in some sense "divine." But they did not use the word "Christ" to make this point, and if we suppose they did we shall radically misunderstand them. Modern book titles such as "Jesus Who Became Christ" or "From Jesus to Christ," which propound the thesis that the human Jesus was divinized after his death, are not only wrong in this thesis, but also perpetuate this linguistic mistake not dissimilar to the simple misreadings of the gospel whereby, for instance, Peter's confession, "You are the Christ," and Caiaphas's question, "Are you the Christ?," are imagined to be confessing, or questioning, Jesus' status as the second person of the Trinity.

The other preliminary disclaimer ought by now to be obvious as well. The word "Christ" is not a proper name. In Western culture, where most people have two basic names by which they are known, it is fatally easy to assume that the phrase "Jesus Christ" contains, as it were, Jesus' Christian name and his surname. I suggest that it would be preferable to translate the phrase as "King Jesus," and indeed such a translation would have prevented us, right off the top, from ever imagining that Jesus was politically irrelevant. But more of this anon.

Though the topic is Christology, I will not primarily consider Jesus' Messiahship. Rather, I have taken as my task to develop the biblical basis for the belief in the divinity of Jesus. To that major task I now turn.

The question must be approached from both sides. First, in what sense, if any, can we meaningfully use the word "god" to talk about the human Jesus, Jesus as he lived, walked, taught, healed, and died in first-century Palestine? In what sense might Jesus conceivably have thought in these terms about himself? Can we, as historians, describe the way in which he might have wrestled with this question within the parameters of his own first-century Jewish worldview? Second, what happens to our sense of the identity of

God himself when we allow our long historical look at Jesus to influence what we mean by that endlessly fascinating word?[1]

1. Asking the Right Question

It is important to begin by clarifying the question. When people ask "Was Jesus God?" they usually think they know what the word "God" means, and are asking whether we can fit Jesus into that. I regard this as deeply misleading. I can perhaps make my point clear by a personal illustration.

For seven years I was college chaplain at Worcester College, Oxford. Each year I used to see the first-year undergraduates individually for a few minutes, to welcome them to the college and make a first acquaintance. Most were happy to meet me; but many commented, often with slight embarrassment, "You won't be seeing much of me; you see, I don't believe in God."

I developed a stock response: "Oh, that's interesting; which god is it you don't believe in?" This used to surprise them; they mostly regarded the word "God" as univocal, always meaning the same thing. So they would stumble out a few phrases about the god they didn't believe in: a being who lived up in the sky, looking down disapprovingly at the world, occasionally "intervening" to do miracles, sending bad people to hell while allowing good people to share his heaven. Again, I had a stock response for this very common statement of "spy-in-the-sky" theology: "Well, I'm not surprised you don't believe in that god. I don't believe in that god either."

At this point the undergraduate would look startled. Then, perhaps, a faint look of recognition; it was sometimes rumored that half the college chaplains at Oxford were atheists. "No," I would say, "I believe in the god I see revealed in Jesus of Nazareth." What most people mean by "god" in late-modern Western culture simply isn't the mainstream Christian meaning.

1. This chapter expands and develops chapter 10 of my forthcoming book with Marcus J. Borg, *The Meaning of Jesus: Two Visions,* to be published by HarperSanFrancisco.

The same is true for meanings of "god" within postmodernity. We are starting to be more aware that many people give allegiance to "gods" and "goddesses" which are personifications of forces of nature and life. An obvious example is the earth-goddess, Gaia, revered by some within the New Age movement. Following the long winter of secularism, in which most people gave up believing in anything "religious" or "spiritual," the current revival of spiritualities of all sorts is an inevitable swing of the pendulum. The swing is actually a cultural shift in which people have been able once more to celebrate dimensions of human existence that the Enlightenment had marginalized. But one cannot assume that what people mean by "god" or "spirit," "religion" or "spirituality," within these movements, bears very much relation to Christianity. I even heard, not long ago, an Italian justifying the pornography which featured his high-profile wife on the grounds that its portrayal of sexuality was deeply "religious." The Pope, he thought, should have welcomed it.

Eros has of course been well known to students of divinities time out of mind. But only when a culture has forgotten, through long disuse, how god-language actually works, could someone assume that the deeply "religious" feelings, evoking a sense of wonder and transcendence, which serious eroticism (and lots of other things) can produce, could be straightforwardly identified with anything in the Judaeo-Christian tradition. Did they never hear of paganism? It is vital that in our generation we inquire once more: to what, or rather whom, does the word "god" truly refer? And if, as Christians, we bring together Jesus and God in some kind of identity, what sort of an answer does that provide to our question?

Even to begin to address these issues, it is vital to consider some notes about the first-century Jewish meanings of the word "god."

2. "God" in First-Century Judaism

What did first-century Jews, including Jesus and his first followers, mean by "god"? This is obviously the place to start. Their belief can be summed up in a single phrase: *creational and covenantal monotheism.*[2] This needs spelling out.

Some theologies, e.g., ancient Epicureanism and modern Deism, believe in a god, or gods, but think they have nothing much to do with the world we live in. Others, like Stoicism, believe that god, or "the divine," or "the sacred," is simply a dimension of the world we live in, so that "god" and the world end up being pretty much the same thing. Both of these can give birth to practical or theoretical atheism. The first can let its "god" get so far away that he disappears; this is what happened with Marx and Feuerbach in the nineteenth century, allowing the "absentee landlord" of eighteenth-century Deism to become simply an absentee. The second can get so used to various "gods" around the place that it ceases to care much about them; this is what happened with a good deal of ancient paganism in Greece and Rome, until, as Pliny wryly remarks, the arrival of Christianity stirred up pagans to a fresh devotion to their gods.[3]

The Jews believed in a quite different "god." This god, YHWH, "the One Who Is," the Sovereign One, was not simply the objectification of forces and drives within the world, but was the *maker* of all that exists. Several biblical books, or parts thereof, are devoted to exploring the difference between YHWH and the pagan idols: Daniel, Isaiah 40–55, and a good many Psalms spring obviously to mind. The theme is summed up in the Jewish daily prayer: "YHWH our God, YHWH is one!"[4]

Classic Jewish monotheism, then, believed that (a) there was one God, who created heaven and earth, and who remained in close and dynamic relation with his creation; and that (b) this God had called Israel to be his special people. This twin belief, tested to the limit and beyond through Israel's checkered career, was characteristically expressed through a particular narrative: the chosen people

2. For full discussion, see my *The New Testament and the People of God*, vol. 1 of *Christian Origins and the Question of God* (Minneapolis: Fortress, 1992), ch. 9.

3. Pliny the Younger, Letters 10.96.9f.

4. Deuteronomy 6:4, the opening words of the prayer known as the *Shema*. There are various other possible ways of translating the underlying Hebrew, e.g., "YHWH our God is one YHWH," or "YHWH is our God, YHWH alone."

were also the *rescued* people, liberated from slavery in Egypt, marked out by the gift of Torah, established in their land, exiled because of disobedience, but promised a glorious return and final settlement. Jewish-style monotheism meant living in this story, trusting in this one true God, the God of creation and covenant, of Exodus and Return.

This God was utterly different from the pantheist's "one god" (this is an important point to note; many, including many scholars, have blithely assumed that because Stoics and others talked about "one god" they were saying the same thing as the Jews). Utterly different, too, from the faraway ultra-transcendent gods of the Epicureans. Always active within his world — did he not feed the young ravens when they called upon him?[5] — he could be trusted to act more specifically on behalf of Israel. His eventual overthrow of pagan power at the political level would be the revelation of his overthrow of the false gods of the nations. His vindication of his people, liberating them finally from all their oppressors, would also be the vindication of his own name, his reputation. In justifying his people, he would himself be justified. In his righteousness, his covenant faithfulness, they would find their own.

This monotheism was never, in our period, an inner analysis of the being of the one God. It was always a way of saying, frequently at great risk: our God is the true God, and your gods are worthless idols. It was a way of holding on to hope. We can see the dynamic of this monotheism working its way out in the sundry and manifold crises of second-temple Judaism, with the Maccabees, Judas the Galilean, and above all the two wars of the late 60s and early 130s AD as the tips of the iceberg, revealing how the creational and covenantal theology and worldview remained at work through the period and in different groups.

This God was both other than the world and continually active within it. The words "transcendent" and "immanent," we should note, are pointers to this double belief, but do not clarify it much. Because this God is thus simultaneously other than his people and present with them, Jews of Jesus' day had developed several ways of

5. Psalm 147:9.

speaking about the activity of this God in which they attempted to hold together, because they dared not separate, these twin truths. Emboldened by deep-rooted traditions, they explored what appears to us a strange, swirling sense of a rhythm of mutual relations within the very being of the one God: a to-and-fro, a give-and-take, a command-and-obey, a sense of love poured out and love received. God's Spirit broods over the waters, God's Word goes forth to produce new life, God's Law guides his people, God's Presence or Glory dwells with them in fiery cloud, in tabernacle and temple. These four ways of speaking moved to and fro from metaphor to trembling reality-claim and back again. They enabled Jews to speak simultaneously of God's sovereign supremacy and his intimate presence, of his unapproachable holiness and his self-giving compassionate love.

Best known of all is perhaps a fifth. God's Wisdom is his handmaid in creation, the firstborn of his works, his chief of staff, his delight. God's Wisdom is another way of talking about God present with his people in the checkered careers of the patriarchs, and particularly in the events of the Exodus: Wisdom becomes closely aligned thereby with Torah and Shekinah.[6] Through the Lady Wisdom of Proverbs 1–8, the creator has fashioned everything, especially the human race. To embrace Wisdom is therefore to discover the secret of being truly human, of reflecting God's image.[7]

3. Monotheism and Early Christology

This rich seam of Jewish thought is where the early Christians went quarrying for language to deal with the phenomena before them. Some have suggested that the impact of Jesus on the early Christians was so huge that they simply ransacked all their vocabulary of glory and splendor to find more and more honorific titles to heap on him, without much reflection on what they were doing. This does not do justice, it seems to me, to what was actually going on.

6. See particularly Wisdom 10–11; Sirach 24.
7. All five, in Hebrew, are represented by feminine nouns.

Some, conversely, have suggested that it was only when the early church started to lose its grip on its Jewish roots, and began to compromise with pagan philosophy, that it could think of Jesus in the same breath as the one God. Jewish polemic has often suggested that the Trinity and the incarnation, those great pillars of patristic theology, are sheer paganization. I shall argue against this view as well. The question can be posed thus: were the New Testament writers, in saying what they did about Jesus, losing touch with the real, historical, earthly, flesh-and-blood Jesus, and, through ascribing something like "divinity" to him, creating a non-earthly "Christ of faith"?

Whatever we say of later Christian theology, in the patristic period for instance, this is certainly not true of the New Testament. Long before secular philosophy and its terminology was invoked to describe the inner being of the one God (and the relation of this God to Jesus and to the Spirit), a vigorous and very Jewish tradition took the language and imagery of Spirit, Word, Law, Presence (and/ or Glory), and Wisdom, and developed them in relation to Jesus of Nazareth and the Spirit. One might think that a sixth was also explored, namely God's Love; except that, for them, God's Love was already no mere personification, a figure of speech for the loving God at work, but a person, the crucified and risen Jesus. There is not space here to explore these themes in detail, but it is important to glance in outline at the way in which different writers developed these ideas.

Several of the Jewish themes I have mentioned come together in the famous Johannine prologue (John 1:1-18). Jesus is here the Word of God; the passage as a whole is closely dependent on the Wisdom tradition, and is thereby closely linked with the Law and the Presence, or Glory, of God. "The Word became flesh, and *tabernacled* in our midst; we saw his *glory*, glory as of God's only son."[8] However much the spreading branches of Johannine theology might hang over the wall, offering fruit to the pagan world around, the roots of the tree are firmly embedded in Jewish soil.

---

8. John 1:14; cp. Sirach 24. On the comparison see my *The New Testament and the People of God*, 413-16.

Similar points can be made about the Letter to the Hebrews. The Christology of the opening verses of the letter is closely reminiscent of the portrait of Wisdom in *Wisdom of Solomon* chapter 7. The letter then, of course, goes its own way, constructing a Christology unique in the New Testament in terms of Jesus as both high priest and sacrifice, as the ultimate reality to which the figure of Melchizedek pointed. Convergence with the rest of early Christianity, however, is provided particularly through the development of the idea of Jesus' divine and Davidic sonship, dependent on such passages as 2 Samuel 7:14;[9] and through Jesus' fulfillment of the prophesied destiny of the whole human race.[10]

John and Hebrews are usually regarded as late. So what about the early material? Paul is our earliest Christian writer, and, interestingly, the earliest parts of his letters may be those which embody or reflect pre-Pauline Christian tradition.

Within that strand of material, three passages stand out.[11] In 1 Corinthians 8:6, within a specifically Jewish-style monotheistic argument, he adapts the *Shema* itself, placing Jesus within it: "For us there is one God — the Father, from whom are all things and we to him; and one Lord, Jesus Christ, through whom are all things and we through him." This is possibly the single most revolutionary christological formulation in the whole of early Christianity, staking out a high Christology founded within the very citadel of Jewish monotheism.

The same is true of Philippians 2:5-11 (often regarded as pre-Pauline; though Paul intends every word to bear weight within the wider letter). Paul this time draws on the fiercely monotheistic theology of Isaiah 40–55 to celebrate Christ's universal lordship: "At the name of Jesus," he declares, "every knee shall bow." Isaiah has YHWH defeating the pagan idols and being enthroned over them; Paul has Jesus exalted to a position of equality with "the Father" be-

---

9. E.g., Hebrews 1:5.

10. E.g., Hebrews 2:5-9; cp. 1 Corinthians 15:27; Ephesians 1:22; Philippians 3:21. All these passages either quote or allude to Psalm 8:4-8, esp. v. 7.

11. For which, see the detailed studies in my *The Climax of the Covenant* (Edinburgh: T & T Clark, 1991; Philadelphia: Fortress, 1992), chs. 4, 5, and 6; and *What St. Paul Really Said* (Oxford: Lion; Grand Rapids: Eerdmans, 1997), ch. 4.

cause he has done what, in Jewish tradition, only the one God can do. It is important to note here that, though Philippians 2:5-11 remains thoroughly within the Jewish world of thought, precisely from that world it confronts the pomp and pagan pretensions of Caesar. The language is reminiscent of imperial acclamation-formulae: Jesus, not Caesar, is the "servant" who is now to be hailed as "lord" and "savior." Jewish monotheistic theology with Jesus himself as its focus, confronting pagan power with what is essentially a Jewish kingdom-of-God theology, which of course goes back to the earthly, human Jesus himself.

Despite its many differences with both 1 Corinthians 8 and Philippians 2, Colossians 1:15-20 belongs firmly on the same map. Its clear poetic structure reveals it to be a Wisdom-poem, exploring the classic Jewish theme that the world's creator is also its redeemer, and vice versa, and thereby confronting the "powers of the world" with the news that their creator and lord is now revealed, made known, and worshipped as the one who has liberated his people from the grip precisely of those "powers."[12] But at every point of creation and redemption, as revealed by this poem, we discover, not Wisdom, but Jesus. The same point is made, by a sort of concentration of this theology into one statement, in the spectacular verse, Colossians 2:9: "In him the whole fullness of deity dwells bodily." We should not underestimate that word *somatikos,* "bodily": Paul intends to speak, not of some disembodied theological cipher, but of the Jesus whose body was killed as the revelation of the love of God, and raised to new life.[13]

Another passage which is very different on the surface and very similar underneath is Galatians 4:1-11. Here Paul tells the story of the world as the story of God's freeing of slaves, and his making them his children, his heirs. As in the Exodus, the true God reveals himself as who he is, putting the idols to shame (4:8-11). But the God who has now revealed himself in this way is the God who "sends the son" (4:4) and then "sends the Spirit of the Son" (4:6). In

---

12. Cf. Colossians 2:14f.

13. Compare the logic of Romans 5:6-11: it is because Jesus is God's son in a fully personal and ontological sense that his death reveals God's love. Adoptionism would make nonsense of Paul's whole central argument at this point.

these passages we have, within thirty years of Jesus' death, what would later be called a very high Christology. It is very early, and very Jewish. The logic of the passage is that the Galatians must either learn to know the one true God in terms of Jesus and the Spirit, or they will be in effect turning back to the principalities and powers to which they were formerly subject. Either incipient trinitarianism or a return to paganism. With this we are, indeed, very near the heart of the biblical basis of Christology; and in terms of dating we are looking at a passage that dates at the outside from twenty-five years after the crucifixion, and quite likely a lot earlier.

Within these passages, and others like them (for instance, the remarkable Romans 8:3-4), Paul, like other New Testament writers, uses the phrase "son of God" to denote Jesus. Later Christian theologians, forgetting their Jewish roots, would of course read this as straightforwardly Nicene Christology: Jesus was the second person of the Trinity. Many have assumed that this is meant by the phrase in John and Hebrews, though that assumption should probably be challenged.[14] Paul's usage, though, is much subtler, and offers further clues not only as to what the earliest Christians believed, but why. "Son of God" in Jewish thought was used occasionally for angels, sometimes for Israel (e.g., Exodus 4:22), and sometimes for the king. These latter uses (such as 2 Samuel 7:14, Psalm 2:7, and Psalm 89:27) were influential both in sectarian Judaism[15] and in early Christianity. Since the early Christians all regarded Jesus as the Messiah of Israel, the one in whom Israel's destiny had been summed up, it is not surprising, whatever language Jesus had or had not used of himself, that they exploited this phrase (it is perhaps too formal, and too redolent of the wrong way of doing New Testament Christology, to call it a "title"), which was available both in their Bible and their surrounding culture, to denote Jesus and to connote his Messiahship.[16]

14. Cf. George B. Caird and L. D. Hurst, *New Testament Theology* (Oxford: Oxford University Press, 1994), 320f. This is not to say, as some have assumed, that the usage is therefore implying an adoptionist Christology.

15. "Son of God" is found as a messianic title at Qumran in 4Q174. The meaning of the same phrase in 4Q246 is disputed.

16. Cf. also Romans 1:3-4, where, though "son of God" means more than "Messiah," it does not mean less.

But already by Paul's day something more was in fact going on. "Son of God" came quickly to be used as a further way, in addition to the five Jewish ways already available and exploited by the early Christians, of saying that what had happened in Jesus was the unique and personal action of the one God of Israel. It became another way of speaking about the one God present, personal, active, saving, and rescuing, while still being able to speak of the one God sovereign, creating, sustaining, sending, remaining beyond. Another way, in fact, of doing what neither Stoicism nor Epicureanism needed to do, and paganism in general could not do, but which Judaism offered what must have seemed a heaven-sent way of doing: holding together the majesty and the compassion of God, the transcendence and the immanence of God, creation and covenant, sovereignty and presence.

All this means, of course, that the phrase "son of God," taken out of context, is not much help for deciding what a particular New Testament writer thought about Jesus. Put back in context, though, it appears as what it is: one focal point of a wide variety of arguments in which the Jewish messianic hope comes together with the Jewish expectation that YHWH himself would be savingly present with his people. If this is not so, Paul's usage is inexplicable: the death of God's son can only reveal God's love (as in, e.g., Romans 5:6-10) if the son is the personal expression of God himself. It will hardly do to say, "I love you so much that I'm going to send someone else."

Similar exegetical points could be made, were there more space, from other New Testament writings, not least the very Jewish Book of Revelation. But I have said enough to indicate, or at least point in the direction of, the remarkable phenomenon at the heart of earliest Christianity. Long before anyone talked about "nature" and "substance," "person" and "Trinity," the early Christians had quietly but definitely discovered that they could say what they felt obliged to say about Jesus (and the Spirit) by telling the Jewish story of God, Israel, and the world, in the Jewish language of Spirit, Word, Torah, Presence/Glory, Wisdom, and now Messiah/Son. It is as though they discovered Jesus within the Jewish monotheistic categories they already had. The categories seemed to have been made for him. They fitted him like a glove. And — this being of course the point within the logic of this chapter and this book — it was the *human* Jesus, the *earthly* Jesus that they fitted. It was not some nebulous "Christ of faith" that these writers were talking about. It was the one and only Jesus himself.

4. The Origin of Christology

This, of course, raises in an acute form the question: why did they tell the story like this? We now work backwards, in the logic of this chapter, from what people said about Jesus a decade or three after his death and resurrection to what can be said about the human, earthly Jesus himself, in his own time, and even, dare we say, in his own mind.

At this point we need to ward off several frequent misunderstandings. I mention only two.

First, it is often supposed that addressing this question involves psychoanalyzing Jesus. It does not. It involves doing what historians always do: inquiring after motivation, worldview beliefs, the things that make characters in the story act as they did.

Second, it is often supposed that the resurrection (whatever we mean by that) somehow "proves" Jesus' "divinity." If this were the case, whatever we said about Jesus' own historical life, and his self-awareness during it, would be ultimately irrelevant. We could still have a (risen) "Christ of faith" separated from the earthly, and perhaps non-divine, "Jesus of history." This seems to me to short-circuit the reasoning that in fact took place. Suppose one of the two brigands crucified alongside Jesus had been raised from the dead. People would have said the world was a very odd place; they would not have said that the brigand was therefore divine. No, the basic meaning of the resurrection, as Paul says in Romans 1:4, was that Jesus was indeed the Messiah. As I have argued elsewhere, this led quickly, within earliest Christianity, to the belief that his death was therefore not a defeat, but a victory, the conquest of the powers of evil and the liberation, the Exodus, of God's people and, in principle, of the world. In Jesus, in other words, Israel's God, the world's creator, had accomplished at last the plan he had been forming ever since the covenant was forged in the first place. In Jesus God had rescued Israel from her suffering and exile. And then the final step: in Jesus God had done what, in the Bible, God had said he would do himself. He had heard the people's cry and come to help them.

Ultimately, then, it is true that Jesus' resurrection led the early church to speak of him within the language of Jewish monotheism. But there was no easy equation. Resurrection pointed to Messiahship; Messiahship, to the task performed on the cross; that task, to the God who had promised to accomplish it himself. From there on it was a matter of rethinking, still very Jewishly, how these things could be.

Does any of this train of thought go back to Jesus himself? I have argued that it does.[17] This is not the same as Jesus' *messianic* vocation. It cannot be read off from the usage of any "titles" such as "son of God" or "son of man." It is not difficult, as I said at the start of this paper, to establish that Jesus of Nazareth believed himself to be Israel's Messiah; but this tells us nothing about whether he believed himself to be in any sense identified with Israel's God. Lots of other people within a hundred years either side of Jesus believed themselves to be God's anointed, and we have no reason to suppose that any of them imagined themselves to be in any sense "divine."[18] No: the case for saying that Jesus thought of himself in a way which stands in continuity, though not identity, with what Paul and the other New Testament writers said about him grows out of Jesus' basic kingdom-proclamation, and out of Jesus' conviction that it was his task and role, his vocation, not only to speak of this kingdom, but also to enact and embody it.

I have argued elsewhere that a central feature of Jewish expectation, and kingdom-expectation at that, in Jesus' time was the hope that YHWH would return in person to Zion. Having abandoned Je-

17. In my *Jesus and the Victory of God* (Minneapolis: Fortress, 1996), ch. 13, to which the following is necessarily and obviously indebted.
18. Though Eusebius and Jerome have an interesting remark about bar-Kochba supposing himself to be a luminary descended from heaven (possibly a wrong deduction from his nickname): Eusebius HE 4.6.2, Jerome ad Rufinum 3.31. See *Jesus and the Victory of God*, 627f., with note 66.

rusalem at the time of the exile, his return was delayed, but he would come back at last. Within this context, someone who told cryptic stories about a king, or a master, who went away, left his servants tasks to perform, and then returned to see how they were getting on must — not "might," *must* — point to this controlling, overarching metanarrative. Of course, the later church, forgetting the first-century Jewish context, read such stories as though they were originally about Jesus himself going away and then returning in a "second coming." Of course, cautious scholars, noticing this, deny that Jesus would have said such things. I propose that here, at the heart of Jesus' work, and at the moment of its climax, Jesus not only told stories about the king who came back to Zion to judge and to save, but he acted as though he thought the stories were coming true *in what he was himself accomplishing.* This is the context, at last, in which I think it best to approach the question with which this paper began. How do we speak appropriately of Jesus, drawing together historical language about Jesus and theological language about God?

It is of course a huge and difficult matter. Caricatures abound (to which the Bible gives no authority): the Jesus who wanders round with a faraway look, listening to the music of the angels, remembering the time when he was sitting up in heaven with the other members of the Trinity, having angels bring him bananas on golden dishes. (I do not wish to caricature the caricatures; but you would be surprised what devout people sometimes believe.) Equally, what passes for historical scholarship sometimes produces an equal and opposite caricature: the Jesus who wandered around totally unreflectively, telling stories without perceiving how they would be heard, announcing God's kingdom, speaking of bringing it about, yet failing to ruminate on his own role within the drama. We must not, as many have done, lose our nerve, and start asking the sorts of questions (e.g., "what sort of a person would think he was divine?") that depend for their rhetorical force on the implied assumption "within our culture." Too many have been content with the cheap retort that anyone supposing himself to be God incarnate must be mad, and we do not think Jesus was mad. As it stands, this invites another fairly obvious retort: some of Jesus' opponents, and some even in his own family, thought he was out of his mind, and it is unlikely in the extreme that the early church made these charges up. But the question is still wrongly put. What we should be asking is: never mind what would count in our culture, how would a first-century Jew have approached and thought about these matters?

There is some evidence — cryptic, difficult to interpret, but evidence nonetheless — that some first-century Jews had already started to explore the meaning of certain texts, not least Daniel 7, which spoke of Israel's God sharing his throne with another (something expressly denied, of course, in Isaiah 42:8).[19] These were not simply bits of speculative theology. They belonged, as more or less everything did at that period, to the whirling world of politics and pressure groups, of agendas and ambitions, all bent on discovering how Israel's God would bring in the kingdom and how best to speed the process on its way. To say that someone would share God's throne was to say that, through this one, Israel's God would win the great decisive victory. This is what, after all, the great Rabbi Akiba seems to have believed about bar-Kochba.

And Jesus seems to have believed it about himself. The language was deeply coded, but the symbolic action was not. He was coming to Zion, doing what YHWH had promised to do. He explained his action with riddles all pointing in the same direction. Recognize this, and you start to see it all over the place, in parables and actions whose other layers have preoccupied us. Why, after all, does Jesus tell a story about a yearning father in order to account for his own behavior?[20] It is this that also accounts for his sovereign attitude to Torah; his speaking on behalf of Wisdom; his announcement of forgiveness of sins.[21] By themselves, none of these would be conclusive. Even if they are allowed to stand as words

19. On throne-imagery, and the idea of sharing God's throne, see *Jesus and the Victory of God*, 624-29.

20. For this, and what follows, see the close listing of material, and the argument, of *Jesus and the Victory of God*, 645-51.

21. Jacob Neusner, in an interview following the publication of his book *A Rabbi Talks with Jesus: An Intermillennial, Interfaith Exchange* (New York: Doubleday, 1993), declared that Jesus' attitude to Torah made him want to ask: "Who do you think you are? God?"

and actions of Jesus, they remain cryptic. But predicate them of the same young man who is then on his way to Jerusalem to confront the powers that be with the message, and the action, of the kingdom of God, and who tells stories as he does so which are best interpreted as stories of YHWH returning to Zion; and you have reached, I believe, the deep heart of Jesus' own sense of vocation. He believed himself called to do and be what, in the scriptures, only Israel's God did and was.

Or suppose we approach the matter from another angle, vital and central but, remarkably enough, frequently overlooked. Jesus' actions during the last week of his life focussed on the temple. Judaism had two great incarnational symbols, temple and Torah: Jesus seems to have believed it was his vocation to upstage the one and outflank the other. Judaism spoke of the presence of her God in her midst, in the pillar of cloud and fire, in the Presence ("Shekinah") in the temple. Jesus acted and spoke as if he thought he were a one-man counter-temple movement. So, too, Judaism believed in a God who was not only high-and-mighty but also compassionate and caring, tending his flock like a shepherd, gathering the lambs in his arms. Jesus used just that God-image, more than once, to explain his own actions. Judaism believed that her God would triumph over the powers of evil, within Israel as well as outside. Jesus spoke of his own coming vindication, after his meeting the Beast in mortal combat. Jesus, too, used the language of the Father sending the Son. The so-called parable of the Wicked Tenants could just as well be the parable of the Son Sent at Last. His awareness, in faith, of the one he called Abba, Father, sustained him in his messianic vocation to Israel, and to act as his Father's personal agent to her.[22] So we could go on. Approach the incarnation from this angle, and it is no category mistake, but the appropriate climax of creation and covenant. Wisdom, God's blueprint for humans, at last herself becomes human. The Shekinah glory turns out to have a human face.

What are we therefore saying about the earthly Jesus? In Jesus himself, I suggest, we see the biblical portrait of YHWH come to life: the loving God, rolling up his sleeves (Isaiah 52:10) to do in person

22. *Jesus and the Victory of God*, 648-50.

the job that no one else could do; the creator God, giving new life; the God who works *through* his created world, and supremely through his human creatures; the faithful God, dwelling in the midst of his people; the stern and tender God, relentlessly opposed to all that destroys or distorts the good creation, and especially human beings, but recklessly loving all those in need and distress. "He shall feed his flock like a shepherd; he shall carry the lambs in his arms; and gently lead those that are with young." It is the Old Testament portrait of YHWH; but it fits Jesus like a glove.

Let me be clear, also, what I am *not* saying. I do not think Jesus "knew he was God" in the same sense that one knows one is tired or happy, male or female. He did not sit back and say to himself, "Well I never! I'm the second person of the Trinity!" Rather, "as part of his human vocation, grasped in faith, sustained in prayer, tested in confrontation, agonized over in further prayer and doubt, and implemented in action, he believed he had to do and be, for Israel and the world, that which according to scripture only YHWH himself could do and be."[23] I commend to you this category of "vocation" as the appropriate way forward for talking about what Jesus knew and believed about himself. This Jesus is both thoroughly credible as a first-century Jew, and thoroughly comprehensible as the one to whom early, high, Jewish Christology looked back.

5. Jesus and Christology Today

There is much more that could be said on the biblical basis of Christology, but space is running out. Let me conclude with some reflections on the implications of all this for how we approach questions of Christology today.

Thinking and speaking of God and Jesus in the same breath is not, as has often been suggested, a category mistake. Of course, if you start with the Deist god and the reductionists' Jesus, they will never fit, but then they were designed not to. Likewise, if you start with the New Age gods-from-below, or for that matter the gods of

---

23. *Jesus and the Victory of God*, 653.

ancient paganism, and ask what would happen if such a god were to become human, you would end up with a figure very different from the one in the Gospels. But if you start with the God of the Exodus, of Isaiah, of creation and covenant, of the Psalms, and ask what that God might look like, were he to become human, you will find that he might look very much like Jesus of Nazareth, and perhaps never more so than when he dies on a Roman cross.

Anyone can, of course, declare that this picture was read back by the early church into Jesus' mind. The evidence for this is not good. The early church did not make much explicit use of the themes I have noted in Jesus' self-understanding; there is, of course, some overlap, but also quite substantial discontinuity. (This, ironically, may be why this latent Christology has often gone unnoticed; scholar and pietist alike have preferred the early church's christological formulations to Jesus' christological vocation, the pietist reading them back into Jesus' mind, the scholar declaring this impossible and then arguing on that basis for an unreflective or reductionist Jesus.) As with Jesus' Messiahship, and his vocation to suffer and die, the key sayings remain cryptic, only coming into focus when grouped around the central symbolic actions. Such riddles only make sense, only find a natural life-setting, within Jesus' own ministry. The early church was not reticent about saying that Jesus was Messiah, that his death was God's saving act, and that he and his Father belonged together within the Jewish picture of the one God.

I see no reason why the contemporary church should be reticent about this either. Using incarnational language about Jesus, and trinitarian language about God, is of course self-involving: it entails a commitment of faith, love, trust, and obedience. But there is a difference between self-involving language and self-referring language. I do not think that when I use language like this about Jesus and God I am merely talking about the state of my own devotion. I think I am talking, self-involvingly of course, about Jesus and God. All this leads, in conclusion, to the area which, it seems to me, is just as vital a part of the contemporary christological task as learning to speak truly about the earthly Jesus and his sense of vocation. We must learn to speak biblically, in the light of this Jesus, about the identity of the one true God. I have no space, of course, to develop this fully: what follows is an attempt to summarize material that could easily turn into a whole other chapter, or more.[24]

I return to what I said at the start of the paper. Western orthodoxy has, it seems to me, for too long had an overly lofty, detached, and (as the feminists would say) kyriarchal view of god. It has always tended to approach the christological question by assuming this view of god, and then by fitting Jesus into it. Hardly surprisingly, the result was a docetic Jesus, which in turn generated the protest of the eighteenth century and historical scholarship since then, not least because of the social and cultural arrangements that the combination of semi-Deism and docetism generated and sustained. That combination remains powerful, not least in parts of my own Anglican Communion, and it still needs a powerful challenge. My proposal is not that we know what the word "god" means, and manage somehow to fit Jesus into that. Instead, I suggest that we think historically about a young Jew, possessed of a desperately risky, indeed apparently crazy, vocation, riding into Jerusalem in tears, denouncing the temple, and dying on a Roman cross — and that we somehow allow our meaning for the word "god" to be recentered around that point.

Let me put it like this. After twenty years of serious historical-Jesus study, I still say the creed *ex animo;* but I now mean something very different by it, not least by the word "god" itself. The portrait has been redrawn. At its heart, as disclosed in the biblical writings, we discover a human face, surrounded by a crown of thorns. God's purpose for Israel has been completed. Salvation is of the Jews, and from the King of the Jews it has come. God's covenant faithfulness has been revealed in the good news of Jesus, bringing salvation for the whole cosmos.

24. What follows is borrowed from my article "A Biblical Portrait of God" in *The Changing Face of God*, Lincoln Lectures in Theology 1996 (Lincoln Studies in Theology 2), ed. N. T. Wright, Keith Ward, and Brian Hebblethwaite (Lincoln, UK: Lincoln Cathedral Publications, 1996), 9-29. I would like to develop these ideas in dialogue with the proposals, in some way similar and in others not, of Marcus J. Borg, *The God We Never Knew: Beyond Dogmatic Religion to a More Authentic Contemporary Faith* (San Francisco: Harper, 1997).

The thing about painting portraits of God is, of course, that if they do their job properly they should become icons. That is, they should invite not just cool appraisal — though the mind must be involved as well as the heart and soul and strength in our response to this God — but worship. That is fair enough, and I believe that this God is worthy of the fullest and richest worship that we can offer. But, as with some icons, not least the famous Rubley painting of the three men visiting Abraham, the focal point of the painting is not at the back of the painting but on the viewer. Once we have glimpsed the true portrait of God, the onus is on us to reflect it: to reflect it as a community, to reflect it as individuals. The image of the true and living God, once revealed in all its glory, is to be reflected, as was always God's intention, into all the world. The mission of the church can be summed up in the phrase "reflected glory," and it is precisely through engaging in the christological task, not as a detached intellectual exercise but as the very heart of our worship, our praying, our thinking, our preaching, and our living, that we are enabled to reflect that glory. When we see, as Paul says, the glory of God in the face of Jesus Christ, and when we rediscover in the Bible the length and breadth of what that phrase means, we see and discover this not for our own benefit, but so that the glory may shine in us and through us, to bring light and life to the world that still waits in darkness and the shadow of death.

Christology: On Learning
from History

ALISTER E. McGRATH

We can look at history in several ways. We can regard it as the repository of the past, something of interest chiefly to those who find modern life difficult and prefer to dwell in that safer and less threatening world. Or we can see it as something from which we can learn. On this view, history can be seen as a vital resource for the Christian church. We have been in certain situations before, and need to learn from the past.[1] Sometimes the church got things right; sometimes not. We are not condemned to face each situation as if it is something new and unfamiliar; at least traces of present debates can be found in the past. On this view, the study of the history of Christian thought is one way of avoiding past errors, and preparing to face the future. "History repeats itself. It has to. Nobody listens the first time round" (Woody Allen).

This is an issue of importance to all Christians. It is, however, of particular significance to Anglicans, who believe firmly in the importance of being rooted in the past.[2] Part of the Anglican heritage

---

1. See Alister E. McGrath, *Historical Theology: An Introduction* (Oxford: Blackwell, 1998).

2. Interestingly, this is one of the issues which distinguishes Anglican evangelicals from their colleagues in other denominations. James I. Packer is a particularly luminous example of an evangelical who regards engagement with the past as

lies in a willingness to take the past seriously, and avoid the sheer arrogance of those who assert that all those unfortunate enough to live before 1950 were doomed to superstitution and ignorance. A willingness to listen to the past, and even to learn from it, comes hard to those who stridently dismiss the past, perhaps because they fear what such an engagement might yield.

My concern in this essay is to explore the relevance of our history to our present — to cast light on the way in which we can learn from the successes and failures of the past. My intention is to explore a number of episodes from the past in which we can see reflections — and sometimes more than that — of our current concerns. I propose to engage with a number of moments of insight, drawn from the rich tradition of Christian reflection on the identity and significance of Jesus Christ, on the basis of my passionate belief that these are illuminating in relation to our present concerns. The agenda lying behind this engagement means that I will not be providing as much historical analysis as might be expected, but will be aiming to identify the lessons that may be learned from it, and the principles that may be applied in consequence.

We begin by immersing ourselves in the world of the first century, as Christianity begins its process of expansion and consolidation in the eastern Mediterranean world, as we examine the way in which Jesus Christ is presented to the world in the Acts of the Apostles.

The Acts of the Apostles: Relating Christ to the Audience

We live in a pluralist world, in which the good news is proclaimed in a world of many faiths and worldviews. It is perhaps useful to remind ourselves that we have been here before. My Oxford colleague, Michael Green, has pointed out these similarities, and their importance to our situation:

---

essential to serious theology. See Alister McGrath, *J. I. Packer: A Biography* (Grand Rapids: Baker, 1998), especially 248-55.

I find it ironic that people object to the proclamation of the Christian gospel these days because so many other faiths jostle on the doorstep of our global village. What's new? The variety of faiths in antiquity was even greater than it is today. And the early Christians, making as they did ultimate claims for Jesus, met the problem of other faiths head-on from the very outset. Their approach was interesting. . . . They did not denounce other faiths. They simply proclaimed Jesus with all the power and persuasiveness at their disposal.[3]

In this section of this essay, I propose to consider the manner in which the early church "proclaimed Jesus," and especially the manner in which they related that proclamation to the situations of their very different audiences. Acts records a series of addresses and apologetic approaches adopted by Paul and other prominent early Christians, especially Peter. Here we find material which is explicitly apologetic in nature. In a series of addresses and incidents, we find Paul and others directly engaging with the ideas and concerns of a number of major social groups. As the narrative of Acts (and, indeed, the history of the early church) makes clear, each of these groups came to be represented in the early church. The apologetic approaches we find illustrated in Acts led to conversions within each of these groupings.

It is my firm belief that we can learn from these early apologetic approaches valuable lessons for how to proclaim Jesus to modern Western culture. They offer us insights into authentically biblical methods of apologetics, as well as strategies for engaging with specific groups which were of major importance to the development of the early church. My approach in this section will be to explore the broad apologetic strategies developed by Peter and Paul in key speeches in Acts, in which they engage directly with the concerns of two significant groups: the Jews and the Greeks. In each case, the concerns and approaches are different. Yet the same Jesus is defended and conveyed. We may begin by exploring the defense and

---

3. Michael Green, *Acts for Today: First-Century Christianity for Twentieth-Century Christians* (London: Hodder & Stoughton, 1993), 38.

commendation of the gospel to the Jewish people set out in Peter's famous Pentecost sermon of Acts 2.[4]

Peter's famous sermon, preached on the Day of Pentecost (Acts 2:14-36), is dominated by the theme that the coming of Jesus — or, to be more precise, the entire economy of salvation, including the resurrection of Jesus of Nazareth and the giving of the Holy Spirit — fulfills Old Testament prophecy. The basic structure of the address is as follows:

- Section 1 (2:14-21): Setting the events of the Day of Pentecost in the light of Old Testament prophecy. The remarkable events which have unfolded before the eyes of this Jewish audience can only be understood in the light of God's promises to his people in the Old Testament — promises which have now been fulfilled.
- Section 2 (2:22-28): The affirmation of the exaltation of Jesus of Nazareth in the light of Old Testament expectations. Once more, the continuity between the Old Testament and the coming of Jesus is demonstrated. The consistent appeal to prophecy (which would have been devoid of significance to a Gentile audience) would have been of the greatest importance to pious Jews.
- Section 3 (2:29-36): The affirmation of the exaltation of Jesus of Nazareth, along with the theological interpretation of this. "This Jesus, whom you crucified," has been made "both Lord and Christ."
- Section 4 (2:37-40): A call to repentance in order to benefit from the salvation which results.

The first point to note is the way in which Peter's apologetic is directly related to themes which were important and comprehensible to a Jewish audience.[5] The expectation of the coming of the Mes-

4. For detailed studies of this major text, see Robert F. Zehnle's classic study, *Peter's Pentecost Discourse: Tradition and Lucan Reinterpretation in Peter's Speeches of Acts 2 and 3* (Nashville: Abingdon, 1971). Although dated in some respects, the work remains an important analysis of the text itself and its underlying strategy.

5. There is a huge literature dealing with the relationship between Christian-

siah (a notoriously complex and multifaceted notion, as recent scholarship has indicated) was (and remains!) significant for Judaism. Peter can be seen doing three things here.

1. He demonstrates that Jesus meets the specific expectations of Israel.
2. He appeals to authorities (here, prophetic passages in the Old Testament) which carried weight with his audience.
3. He uses language and terminology which would readily have been accepted and understood by his audience. Note in particular his specific reference to Jesus as "Lord and Christ." No explanation is offered, or necessary. These were terms well familiar to his audience. What was new about Peter's message was his emphatic insistence that Jesus was to be identified with both these figures on the basis of his exaltation through God having raised him from the dead.

These are very basic observations, and lack the sophistication which some of us like to adopt in our theologizing. But I happen to believe that, simple though they are, they are also of the utmost importance. I shall return to their application later; let me now move on to look at another audience of major importance in the New Testament period — the Greeks.

It is firmly accepted that one of the most important audiences for the gospel proclamation were "the Greeks." In Paul's first letter to the Corinthians, "the Greeks" are set alongside "the Jews" as a defining group of considerable importance (1 Corinthians 1:22). It is quite clear that Acts shows at least some degree of familiarity and af-

---

ity and Judaism at this early stage in its development. See in particular the enormously important works of N. T. Wright, such as his *The Climax of the Covenant: Christ and the Law in Pauline Theology* (Edinburgh: T. & T. Clark); and *The New Testament and the People of God* (Minneapolis: Fortress). See also J. D. G. Dunn, *Jesus, Paul and the Law* (Louisville: Westminster/John Knox, 1990); J. Gager, *The Origins of Anti-Semitism: Attitudes Towards Judaism in Pagan and Christian Antiquity* (New York: Oxford University Press, 1983); Martin Hengel, *Judaism and Hellenism* (Philadelphia: Fortress, 1981); and G. Vermes, *Jesus and the World of Judaism* (Philadelphia: Fortress, 1984).

finity with Hellenistic rhetoric,[6] as well as the beliefs and practices of classical paganism. So how is the gospel presented in such situations?

It is widely thought that one of the most important descriptions of the early confrontation between Christianity and classical paganism is found in Paul's Areopagus address at Athens (Acts 17:16-34). Paul opens this address with a gradual introduction of the theme of the living God. He does not presuppose familiarity with the idea of the one, true, and living God of Israel. When Paul or Peter addressed Jewish audiences, this concept could be taken for granted; the purpose of the address was to show how Jesus of Nazareth altered matters in a radical manner, and how faith in Jesus was necessary to benefit from his coming.

Here (as in Paul's address to the people of Lystra, Acts 14:15-17), however, no such pre-understanding can be assumed. The basic theme of a living personal God requires introduction before the fundamental themes of the gospel can be enunciated. This simple observation is of considerable apologetic importance, as we shall see.

The difficulty with which we are faced today is that some of the people to whom we wish to preach the gospel have only the most rudimentary understanding of Christianity. Everything needs to be introduced and explained. We can assume very little knowledge of Christian ideas, words, and meanings on the part of many of those we will be dealing with. Paul, sensitive to the simple fact that Greek pagan religion had relatively little to say concerning a living personal God, sets about introducing and explaining the idea.

But notice also that he aims to build on their existing understanding of things. In other words, he identifies aspects of their beliefs which can act as "points of contact" for their grasping at least something of the significance of Jesus. There is a sense in which this sermon may be seen as an illustration of Paul's desire to "be all things to all people" in action. He deliberately identifies the aspects of the gospel which are most likely to find sympathy with his audience, with a view to building on these subsequently. Paul declares

6. See W. S. Kurz, "Hellenistic Rhetoric in the Christological Proofs of Luke-Acts," *Catholic Biblical Quarterly* 42 (1980): 171-95.

that the Athenians are noted for their religiosity; he therefore aims to build on this interest. The religious and philosophical curiosity of the Athenians shaped the contours of his theological exposition. The "sense of divinity" present in each individual is here used as a powerful apologetic device, by which Paul is able to base himself upon acceptable Greek theistic assumptions, while at the same time going beyond them.[7] Paul shows a clear appreciation of the apologetic potential of Stoic philosophy, portraying the gospel as resonating with central Stoic concerns, while extending the limits of what might be known. What the Greeks held to be unknown, possibly unknowable, Paul proclaims to have been made known through the resurrection of Christ. The entire episode illustrates the manner in which Paul is able to exploit the situation of his audience, without compromising the integrity of faith.

The fundamental point being made is that a deity of whom the Greeks had some implicit or intuitive awareness is being made known to them by name and in full, in a manner which can save and not simply inform. The god who is known indirectly through his creation can be known fully in redemption. Notice how Paul explicitly appeals to the idea of creation as a basis for his apologetic approach. Paul here seems to use the theme of creation as a *praeparatio evangelica*, a way of introducing the theme of redemption in Christ. Paul believed passionately in the theological truth and apologetic importance of this insight (Romans 1–2). If Paul is right, it should not be the cause for amazement that we can discern "signals of transcendence" (Peter Berger) within human life. If there is some point of contact already in existence, then apologetics does not need to establish the foundations of the Christian knowledge of God; it can make use of a God-given starting point, within the very nature of the created order itself. The witness to God within his creation can act as a trigger, stimulating people to ask questions about the meaning of life and the identity of Jesus Christ.[8]

7. See Bertil Gartner, *The Areopagus Speech and Natural Revelation* (Uppsala: Gleerup, 1955).

8. For further exploration of this important issue, see Alister E. McGrath, *Intellectuals Don't Need God and Other Modern Myths* (Grand Rapids: Zondervan, 1993), 15-48.

It has been my concern to explore the continuing relevance of the addresses concerning the identity and significance of Jesus recorded in the Acts of the Apostles for the modern church. Given the limits of space, I have only had time to consider briefly two such addresses. However, some general principles may be discerned.

1. Address the audience! The two addresses we have chosen to explore have very different audiences in mind. For example, Peter addressed Jews deeply versed in the Old Testament, and aware of the hopes of Judaism; at Athens, Paul addressed the interests of secular Greek paganism. In each case, the approach adopted is tailored to the particularities of that audience. We need to show that same ability to take the trouble to relate the unchanging gospel of Jesus Christ to the very differing needs of the groups to whom we will minister and preach. The pastor who has one standard apologetic or evangelistic address, which is used time and time again — irrespective of the audience! — is failing to do justice to the gospel.

2. My second point is related to this. *Identify the authorities which carry weight with the audience.* Peter makes an appeal to the Old Testament, knowing that this will be regarded as authoritative by his Jewish audience; Paul appeals to Greek poets as he seeks to defend the gospel. As we seek to proclaim Christ, we need to be sensitive to the intellectual and cultural dynamics of our audience.

3. It is important to use *lines of argument* which will carry weight for our audiences. Peter's careful analysis of the relation of Jesus to the Old Testament expectations is an example of the general principle of trying to ensure that the truth of the gospel is presented in the most effective manner for each audience we address.

But perhaps my most important conclusion is also the simplest — that the apologetic methods adopted in the first period of the expansion of the Christian church can continue to serve, stimulate, and sustain the church of today as it seeks to proclaim Christ in a pluralist culture.

Tradition: Irenaeus — and His Relevance for Today's Individualist Approach to Things

Having considered some of the approaches to the proclamation of Jesus which we encounter in the Acts of the Apostles, I now wish to move on and look at the importance of tradition — that is, the settled convictions of the Christian church — in our understanding of the identity of Jesus Christ. Perhaps the most illuminating episode to cast light on this important theme is the controversy between Irenaeus and Gnosticism in the late second century.[9]

At this stage, Irenaeus was faced with a number of highly speculative, intellectually challenging, and culturally adapted views of the identity of Jesus, emanating from Gnostic sources. Although these views of Jesus made use of biblical passages, and professed to take the New Testament with great seriousness, the views in question bore little relation to the teaching of the church. Irenaeus laid down the centrality of the consensus of the Christian church in relation to the identity of Jesus. The true Christian understanding of the identity and significance of Jesus was safeguarded within the Christian community of faith, and reinforced by its creeds. It was unacceptable for individuals to pronounce what was — or was not — the "Christian" view on this matter; that was not to be determined by such individuals, especially those who were outside the community of faith. Bishops are to be public representatives of this tradition, who swear to remain faithful to the received tradition concerning the identity of Jesus as a condition of their office.

In our own day, we face themes familiar to Irenaeus. For example, we have publicity-seeking bishops, who trade on their episcopal credentials to publicize their books debunking Jesus, alongside others from outside the faith who believe that they have insights which will discredit two millennia of Christian tradition.[10] It is helpful to be reminded that this is not the first time that this has happened,

---

9. See Jacques Fantino, *La théologie d'Irénée: lecture des Écritures en réponse à l'exégèse gnostique: une approche trinitaire* (Paris: Editions du Cerf, 1994). More generally, see Robert M. Grant, *Irenaeus of Lyons* (London: Routledge, 1997).

10. See the useful analysis in N. T. Wright, *Who Was Jesus?* (Grand Rapids: Eerdmans, 1992).

just as it is important to recall the stabilizing role of tradition. Tradition functions as a safeguard, defending us against christological novelties which may sell books yet have no living connection with the Christian community. Anglicanism, with its strong emphasis on the importance of tradition, has every right to insist that the consensus of the past be taken into consideration in weighing the issues in contemporary debates.

The Apologists: Relating Christ and the Gospel to Contemporary Culture

Our third case study also comes from the second century, and focusses on the issue of relating Christianity to the cultural environment in which the Christian community is situated. The apologists of the second century, particularly Justin Martyr, regarded it as essential to establish a dialogue between Christianity and the local intellectual context, on account of the need to proclaim the gospel in that region.

In the case of Justin Martyr, the intellectual background was shaped by the Platonic tradition.[11] Justin's task was thus to use Platonic categories and terms as a vehicle for the communication of the Christian understanding of the identity and importance of Jesus to his secular audience. That task remains important. Perhaps our audiences today may be pragmatic rather than Platonic, and sympathetic to postmodernity rather than the *philosophia perennis*. Yet the challenge remains the same — to communicate the Christian gospel effectively yet faithfully, using a "borrowed" language.

Justin's successes remain an inspiration; nevertheless, his method also raises a difficulty, which would beset the Christian church throughout its long dialogue with the Hellenistic philosophical tradition. To borrow someone else's language and categories may assist communication with that person; it may also, however, have the unintended consequence of subtly altering the content of what is communicated. Adolf von Harnack is an example of a noted scholar of early

---

11. See Henry Chadwick, *Early Christian Thought and the Classical Tradition* (Oxford: Clarendon Press, 1984).

Christianity who drew the conclusion that Christianity became more deeply influenced by Hellenism than it realized, and argued for a process of "de-Hellenization" of Christian thought.[12] While it is possible to argue that Harnack's criticisms are perhaps excessively stringent,[13] the point which he raises seems unassailable. It is all too easy to incorporate, by accident rather than intention, at least some elements of a worldview in seeking to communicate within that worldview.

Justin thus allows us to set two points side by side, one acting as a positive stimulus, the other as a caution:

1. Part of the perennial task of the Christian church is to seek to explain and communicate the relevance of Christ to the world using a vocabulary that the world can understand, and to which it can relate.
2. Part of the perennial danger to which the Christian church is prone is that of incorporating extra-Christian ideas and assumptions into its theological reflection, as an unintended consequence of its attempts to engage and communicate with its audience.

Arius: The Issues, and
What Can Be Learned from Them

One controversy of especial importance to the formation of the definitive Christian statement of the identity of Jesus broke out in the fourth century, and is known as the "Arian controversy." This controversy, which focussed on the teaching of the writer Arius, remains a landmark in the development of classical Christology, and therefore needs to be considered in a little detail.[14]

12. See E. P. Meijering, *Die Hellenisierung des Christentums im Urteil Adolf von Harnacks* (Amsterdam: North Holland, 1985).
13. E.g., see Alister E. McGrath, *The Genesis of Doctrine* (Grand Rapids: Eerdmans, 1997), 145-51.
14. For a much fuller account of the Arian controversy, and invaluable reflections on its continuing significance, see Rowan Williams, *Arius: Heresy and Tradition* (London: DLT, 1987).

Arius emphasized the self-subsistence of God. God is the one and only source of all created things; nothing exists which does not ultimately derive from God. This view of God, which many commentators have suggested is due more to Hellenistic philosophy than to Christian theology, clearly raises the question of the relation of the Father to the Son. Arius regarded the Father as existing before the Son. "There was when he was not," to quote one of Arius's fighting slogans. This decisive affirmation places Father and Son on different levels, and is consistent with Arius's rigorous insistence that the Son is a creature. Only the Father is "unbegotten"; the Son, like all other creatures, derives from this one source of being. However, Arius was careful to emphasize that the Son is unlike every other creature. There is a distinction of rank between the Son and other creatures, including human beings. Arius had some difficulty in identifying the precise nature of this distinction. The Son, he argued, is "a perfect creature, yet not as one among other creatures; a begotten being, yet not as one among other begotten beings." The implication seems to be that the Son outranks other creatures, while sharing their essentially created and begotten nature.

An important aspect of Arius's distinction between Father and Son concerns the unknowability of God. Arius emphasized the utter transcendence and inaccessibility of God. God cannot be known by any other creature. Yet, as we noted above, the Son is to be regarded as a creature, however elevated above all other creatures. Arius pressed home his logic, arguing that the Son cannot know the Father. "The one who has a beginning is in no position to comprehend or lay hold of the one who has no beginning." This important affirmation rests upon the radical distinction between Father and Son. Such is the gulf fixed between them, that the latter cannot know the former unaided. In common with all other creatures, the Son is dependent upon the grace of God if the Son is to perform whatever function has been ascribed to him. It is considerations such as these which led Arius's critics to argue that, at the levels of revelation and salvation, the Son is in precisely the same position as other creatures.

But what about the many biblical passages which seem to suggest that the Son is far more than a mere creature? Arius's opponents were easily able to bring forward a series of biblical passages, pointing to the fundamental unity between Father and Son. On the basis of the controversial literature of the period, it is clear that the Fourth Gospel was of major importance to this controversy, with John 3:35, 10:30, 12:27, 14:10, 17:3, and 17:11 being discussed frequently. Arius's reponse to such texts is significant: the language of "sonship" is variegated in character, and metaphorical in nature. To refer to the "Son" is an honorific, rather than theologically precise, way of speaking. Although Jesus Christ is referred to as "Son" in Scripture, this metaphorical way of speaking is subject to the controlling principle of a God who is totally different in essence from all created beings — including the Son.

The basic elements of Arius's position can be summarized in the following manner. The Son is a creature, who, like all other creatures, derives from the will of God. The term "Son" is thus a metaphor, an honorific term intended to underscore the rank of the Son among other creatures. It does not imply that Father and Son share the same being or status.

Athanasius had little time for Arius's subtle distinctions. If the Son is a creature, then the Son is a creature like any other creature, including human beings. After all, what other kind of creaturehood is there? For Athanasius, the affirmation of the creaturehood of the Son had two decisive consequences, each of which had uniformly negative implications for Arianism.

First, Athanasius made the point that it is only God who can save. God, and God alone, can break the power of sin, and bring us to eternal life. An essential feature of being a creature is that one requires to be redeemed. No creature can save another creature. Only the creator can redeem the creation. Having emphasized that it is God alone who can save, Athanasius then made the logical move which the Arians found difficult to counter. The New Testament and the Christian liturgical tradition alike regard Jesus Christ as Savior. Yet, as Athanasius emphasized, only God can save. So how are we to make sense of this?

The only possible solution, Athanasius argued, is to accept that Jesus is God incarnate. The logic of his argument at times goes something like this:

1. No creature can redeem another creature.
2. According to Arius, Jesus Christ is a creature.
3. Therefore, according to Arius, Jesus Christ cannot redeem humanity.

At times, a slightly different style of argument can be discerned, resting upon the statements of Scripture and the Christian liturgical tradition. The way in which Christians worship is of major importance to the way in which they think.

1. Only God can save.
2. Jesus Christ saves.
3. Therefore Jesus Christ is God.

Salvation, for Athanasius, involves divine intervention. Athanasius thus draws out the meaning of John 1:14 by arguing that the "word became flesh": in other words, God entered into our human situation in order to change it.

The second point that Athanasius made is that Christians worship and pray to Jesus Christ. This represents an excellent case study of the importance of Christian practices of worship and prayer for Christian theology. By the fourth century, prayer to and adoration of Christ were standard features of the way in which public worship took place. Athanasius argued that if Jesus Christ is a creature, then Christians are guilty of worshipping a creature instead of God — in other words, they had lapsed into idolatry. Christians, Athanasius stressed, are totally forbidden to worship anyone or anything except God himself. Athanasius thus argued that Arius seemed to be guilty of making nonsense of the way in which Christians prayed and worshipped. Athanasius argued that Christians were right to worship and adore Jesus Christ, because by doing so, they were recognizing him for what he was — God incarnate.

The Arian controversy had to be settled somehow, if peace was to be established within the church. Debate came to center upon two terms as possible descriptions of the relation of the Father to the Son. The term *homoiousios*, "of like substance" or "of like being," was seen by many as representing a judicious compromise, allowing the proximity between Father and Son to be asserted without requiring any further speculation on the precise nature of their relation. However, the rival term *homoousios,* "of the same substance" or "of the same being," eventually gained the upper hand. Though differing by only one letter from the alternative term, it embodied a very different understanding of the relationship between Father and Son.

So what is the relevance of this debate? In part, it can be suggested that the debate illustrates the dangers of allowing absolute philosophical presuppositions to determine a theological agenda. Arius's presuppositions rule out the Athanasian position as a matter of principle. Yet those philosophical presuppositions are themselves a matter of debate. We can see precisely the same trend today. For example, consider the recent book, *Why Christianity Must Change or Die* by Bishop Spong, which sets out a series of demands which must be met, in his view, if Christianity is to survive.[15]

Spong opens his diatribe against traditional Christianity with an absolute and unqualified statement: "Theism, as a way of defining God, is dead." This sounds rather like the kind of material produced by John Robinson back in the 1960s; indeed, much of Spong's material seems to have its origins in the restlessness of that heady period in Western culture. Yet things have changed rather since the 1960s. Theism is dead? Church attendance figures in the United States hardly bear that out; there has been no kind of slump in church attendance — except in Spong's own diocese. This hardly bodes well for Spong's demand for change or death. If his own diocese is the laboratory for the new religion emerging from this puzzling bishop, we may safely say that the solution offered by Spong has little going for it. Nevertheless, it is important to note how a philosophical presupposition (albeit one which would be vigorously contested by philosophers of religion such as Richard Swinburne, Alvin Plantinga, and Nicholas Wolterstorff) is allowed to assume pole position in Spong's theological argument.

In more general terms, however, the Arian controversy reveals

15. John Shelby Spong, *Why Christianity Must Change or Die: A Bishop Speaks to Believers in Exile* (San Francisco: Harper, 1998).

how three cardinal Christian convictions concerning Jesus need to be upheld and maintained, even in the face of philosophical suspicion and cultural pressure to downgrade Christology to Jesuology. These are:

1. Jesus reveals God;
2. Jesus saves;
3. Jesus is to be worshipped.

These three convictions are the lodestars of orthodox Christology, and are firmly embodied in the traditional teaching and liturgy of Anglicanism. It is essential that they remain so, and that they continue to nourish and safeguard our understanding of the identity and significance of Jesus.

The Reformation: No Debate!

It may, at first sight, appear slightly bizarre to turn to the Reformation as a case study in relation to christological debates. Christology was not an issue of major importance at the time of the Reformation, either as a matter of debate between the Reformers and their Catholic opponents, or between the Reformers themselves.[16] So what can be learned from this?

The Reformation addresses a series of major issues, such as the nature of the true church and the issue of justification by faith, which were seen as central to the identity and mission of the Christian church. Yet amidst all the many issues on which controversy raged in the sixteenth century, the issue of the identity and significance of Jesus was not seen as constitutive in the various divisions which opened up within the medieval church.

16. See Alister E. McGrath, *Reformation Thought: An Introduction,* 2nd ed. (Oxford: Blackwell, 1993). I do not, of course, mean that there were no *differences* between the Reformers: for example, Luther towards the more Alexandrian and Zwingli towards the more Antiochene end of the christological spectrum. My point is rather that these differences were seen as *adiaphora,* matters on which divergence could be accepted.

This simple observation has two major implications. First, it shows that Protestants and Roman Catholics can unite in their defense of the orthodox view of the identity of Christ. While they might differ on other matters, this is a common theme which they may unite in defending against modern criticisms, particularly from those who argue that we would all be advantaged if Christianity were to declare that Jesus Christ was simply a good religious teacher, who took his due (yet limited) place among the countless other aspirants to such a role. This kind of consideration has been enormously important in the thinking of those who have participated in the "Evangelicals and Catholics Together" movement since its inception.[17] Trans-denominational collaboration on fundamental issues of basic Christian orthodoxy is thus an important rallying point in the agenda for the future of Christianity.

In the second place, this consideration is also of importance for Anglicanism, which contains within its ample breadth those who are sympathetic to both sides of the Reformation controversy. Evangelical Anglicans and Anglo-Catholics will continue to argue over the role of the episcopacy, the nature of ordination, and the function of the sacraments. Yet they will be able to unite around the classic Chalcedonian definition of the identity of Christ. Perhaps that union rests upon differing approaches, with evangelicals arguing for the primacy of Scripture in this matter, and Anglo-Catholics preferring to place the emphasis upon the role of tradition, and particularly the Vincentian canon. But the fundamental point remains: in the struggle for the soul of Anglicanism which has broken out since the Lambeth Conference of 1998, Chalcedon holds both a political and theological key to the restoration of orthodoxy.

The Enlightenment: The Rewriting of the Past

We turn now to the dawn of the modern era, as we consider the rise of rationalism and its impact upon Western Christianity. Both De-

17. See Charles Colson and Richard J. Neuhaus, eds., *Evangelicals and Catholics Together: Toward a Common Mission* (Dallas: Word, 1995).

ism and the German Enlightenment developed the thesis that there was a serious discrepancy between the real Jesus of history and the New Testament interpretation of his significance. Underlying the New Testament portrait of the supernatural redeemer of humanity lurked a simple human figure, a glorified teacher of common sense. While a supernatural redeemer was unacceptable to Enlightenment rationalism, the idea of an enlightened moral teacher was not. This idea, developed with particular rigor by H. S. Reimarus, suggested that it was possible to go behind the New Testament accounts of Christ as savior, and uncover a simpler, more human Jesus, who would be acceptable to the new spirit of the age. And so the quest for the real and more credible "Jesus of history" began. Although this quest would ultimately end in failure, the later Enlightenment regarded this "quest" as holding the key to the credibility of Jesus within the context of a rational natural religion. Jesus' moral authority resided in the quality of his teaching and religious personality, rather than in the unacceptable orthodox suggestion that he was God incarnate.

This point was made forcefully by Immanuel Kant, both in his *Religion within the Limits of Reason Alone,* and his celebrated work on the basis of human morality, *Grundlegung zur Metaphysik der Sitten* ("Fundamental Principles of the Metaphysics of Morals"). It is reason and its associated ideals of moral perfection which are authoritative in matters of religion. Christ cannot be allowed to establish ideals of morality (which would compromise the autonomy of human reason, in that it would amount to the imposition of standards of morality upon it). Rather, he has authority only to the extent that he reflects those moral ideals which are themselves grounded in human reason. "Even the Holy One of the gospel must first be compared with our ideal of moral perfection before we can recognize him as such." This outlook has been the subject of considerable criticism, not least on account of its radical individualism, which elevates the subjective consciousness of the individual to the place of a theological norm.

A second area of importance in which orthodox doctrines concerning Jesus were challenged related to the significance of his death. The orthodox approach to Jesus' death on the cross was to interpret it from the standpoint of the resurrection (which the Enlightenment was not prepared to accept as an historical event) as a way in which God was able to forgive the sins of humanity. The Enlightenment subjected this "theory of the atonement" to increasing criticism, as involving arbitrary and unacceptable hypotheses such as original sin. Jesus' death on the cross was reinterpreted in terms of a supreme moral example of self-giving and dedication, intended to inspire similar dedication and self-giving on the part of his followers. Where orthodox Christianity tended to treat Jesus' death (and resurrection) as possessing greater inherent importance than his religious teaching, the Enlightenment marginalized his death and denied his resurrection, in order to emphasize the quality of his moral teaching.

The Enlightenment has gradually receded in importance. Yet the "Quest of the Historical Jesus" remains with us, not least in the form of the "Jesus Seminar." The Enlightenment, refusing to accept the traditional Christian position, chose to impose an alien framework upon Scripture. For example, on the basis of the thoroughly rationalist presuppositions of the late eighteenth century, it argued that Jesus could not have been raised from the dead. Therefore, the Enlightenment concluded, those New Testament passages which spoke of his resurrection could not be believed, and were to be treated either as misunderstandings or misrepresentations. In each case, reconstruction was necessary.

The Enlightenment critique of traditional Christianity thus moved relentlessly from its dogmatic presuppositions to its predetermined conclusions. Its argument was ultimately circular, in that its conclusion was really its controlling presupposition.

So what can be learned from this? Perhaps the most obvious point of all is that the presuppositions which we bring to Scripture determine, in part, our conclusions. Western culture continues to be dominated by a series of assumptions which are inconsistent with at least part of the Christian understanding of Jesus. If the New Testament is read in the light of these assumptions, it should not surprise us to find that they are echoed in the conclusions reached. This pattern is repeatedly found in Bishop Spong's writings, virtually all of which have prominent subtitles informing us that a bishop is rethinking something or other. This much-vaunted "rethinking" generally seems to take place on the basis of a set of rigid presuppositions reflecting the cultural world which the bishop inhabits, and which assume a normative role in his interpretation of the Bible. The outcome of this process of "rethinking" should not surprise us. We have been here before.

Westernization of Jesus: Lambeth

Finally, I turn to an issue which became of major importance since the 1998 Lambeth Conference, although it has been clear for some time that it was due to assume pivotal significance. I refer to the numerical dominance within Anglicanism of the African and Asian provinces, which vigorously contest the Westernization of Jesus. A substantial part of the agenda of Christian writers throughout the non-Western world has been the liberation of Christianity from its Western matrix. Uganda and India, in different ways, represent excellent cases in point.[18] The basic issue here is that of constructing a "local theology," in which the "seed of faith is allowed to interact with the native soil, leading to a new flowering of Christianity, faithful both to the local culture and to the apostolic faith."[19] Theological reflection in the West, including its attempts to make sense of the biblical witness to Christ, is thus constrained and shaped by Western assumptions, and can thus be quite inappropriate outside that context. Timothy E. Yates notes this point as follows:

> Much of the liveliest Anglican life exists in Africa south of the Sahara, in Asia and in Latin America. These voices will claim a hearing increasingly in Anglican consultations and may act as a healthy corrective to the Anglicanism of the comparatively settled, wealthy and arid north, arid in the view of many of these communities because

18. See P. Chenchiah, *Rethinking Christianity in India* (Madras: Sudarisanam, 1938); Charles Nyamiti, *African Theology: Its Problems, Nature and Methods* (Kampala: Gaba Institute, 1971).

19. Robert J. Schreiter, *Constructing Local Theologies* (Maryknoll, NY: Orbis, 1986), 11.

of what is perceived as an over-intellectualized theological tradition and a weakened spirituality.[20]

The conflict of a liberal Western cultural agenda with that of Africa and Asia became obvious at Lambeth 1998. This raises a point of immense christological importance, which I shall state in the form of a highly pointed question: which section of Anglicanism has the right to impose its view of Jesus upon others? It is quite clear that many Western liberal bishops believed that their sophisticated ways of interpreting Scripture and understanding Jesus were vastly superior to the rather primitive views (which at least one unwise Western bishop dismissed as "one step removed from animism") which they encountered among their African and Asian colleagues. These colleagues, for their part, regarded the views of some Westerners as being little more than culturally accommodated views of Jesus, little more than pale reflections of the *Zeitgeist*.

Analysis of Lambeth '98 will continue for many years; in my view, its greatest significance lies in the fact that it publicly demonstrated the massive shift in theological and demographical influence from the West to the emerging world. Yet this shift raises the critically important question: will this new phase in Anglican history, characterized by numerical expansion and a shift south and east from the traditional Anglican spheres of influence, lead to the liberation of Jesus from the bonds which Western thinking has placed upon him? We shall have to wait and see; the omens, however, are promising.

Conclusion

My theme in this essay has been that we can learn from the past. We need to allow ourselves to be challenged, nourished, and excited by the insights of the past. To take the past seriously is to be alive to the fact that others who lived before us may be our critics as much as

20. T. E. Yates, "Anglicans and Mission," in *The Study of Anglicanism*, ed. Stephen Sykes and John Booty (Minneapolis: Augsburg/Fortress Press, 1988), 429-41; quote at 441.

our allies, and call our thinking into question as much as support it. This does not mean for one moment that we are under an obligation to repeat, like a theological parrot, everything that the past has affirmed.[21] "An ancient tradition can be just an old mistake" (Cyprian of Carthage). At points, we will need to insist that our predecessors, for reasons which we can charitably understand, made mistakes for thoroughly laudable reasons. Yet the point remains: we can learn from both the successes and failures of the past.

This essay argues that the past illuminates the present, by letting us see our own christological concerns and strategies in a much broader context. Some of the debates of the present bear a remarkable similarity to those of centuries ago. Perhaps we could do worse than revisit that past, and find in it a stimulus to our own thinking. Above all, it will challenge that most arrogant of all judgments that a theologian may make — that the present is, by definition, more enlightened than the past.

21. See the *bon mot* of Jaroslav Pelikan: "Tradition is the living faith of the dead; traditionalism is the dead faith of the living." Jaroslav Pelikan, *The Vindication of Tradition* (New Haven, CT: Yale University Press, 1984), 65.

The Biblical Christ
in a Pagan Culture

ALAN R. CRIPPEN II

I write this paper from a particular perspective: as a brother in Christ, a fellow Anglican, a husband and father who is struggling to impart the faith of our fathers, a holy faith, to our four beautiful children. From this perspective, my observation is that we live in a culture that is at best blind and at worst hostile to transcendence, truth, and tradition. Almost everything that American mass culture mediates to our family impairs our efforts to be disciples of Jesus Christ. In this struggle however, I am happy to share with you that my wife and I are not alone. We have the support and encouragement of a strong vibrant evangelical parish, Truro Episcopal Church in Fairfax, Virginia, and a supporting network of friends.

I also write as one privileged to be making a living on my livelihood. In other words, I am paid to do what I love to do. By both calling and profession, I am a teacher. In this capacity, I work in a Washington, D.C.-based Christian public policy research and education organization. My activities there involve directing an academic internship program for college-age students who desire to bring their Christian faith to bear on public discourse and debate about national and international politics in Washington.

I share these personal notes with you to say that my approach to the topic of Christ and culture will be from a practitioner's perspective. I wrestle with these issues as a husband, father, teacher, and parishioner. Theoretically, I don't know what more could be said that has not already been said sometime and somewhere before. My own theoretical views on the subject at hand have been shaped by thinkers like Francis Schaeffer, J. Gresham Machen, Abraham Kuyper, H. Richard Niebuhr, Christopher Dawson, and T. S. Eliot; all of whom draw heavily upon St. Augustine. Therefore, to address the topic of "A Biblical Christ in a Pagan Culture" is to revisit a perennial question, what Niebuhr called "the enduring problem." Specifically, what is the relationship of the trinitarian Christ of the Bible to culture in general and to pagan culture in particular? Practically, given this question, the follow-up question is, how should we then live? As a people of God, as the body of Christ, as the holy catholic church, and as "that branch of the same planted by God in this land," how are we to be "in the world, but not of the world"? My hope in addressing these questions is to offer some practical insights and applications with respect to our current philosophical, theological, ecclesiastical, historical, and sociological climate.

The Biblical Christ

You have already read in this volume some of the best minds on the subject of the biblical Christ. Therefore, it seems fitting for me to briefly revisit Niebuhr's construct as it applies to a biblical Christology. In his 1951 classic *Christ and Culture,* Niebuhr outlines five typical responses to the relationship between Christ and culture. Fundamental opposition between Christ and culture characterizes the first response, "Christ-against-culture." Abandonment of the world and the creation of a new intentionally Christian counterculture as advocated by various monastic orders and sectarian movements throughout history, typify this approach to pagan culture. More recently the late John Howard Yoder's *The Politics of Jesus* and Stanley Hauerwas and William Willimon's *Resident*

Aliens: Life in the Christian Colony offer contemporary applications of this response.[1]

All of these authors welcome the end of Christendom. In their view Christendom is the Constantinian "notion that the church needs some sort of surrounding 'Christian' culture to prop it up and mold its young. . . ."[2] This synthesis of church and world accommodated the gospel "ethic of Jesus" to a largely non-Christian society. In the process the "Messianic ethic" was corrupted by capitulation to the social and political ethics of the world. Yoder's "ethic of imitation" demands "radical political action." Or as Hauerwas is wont to say, the church "does not have a social ethic; the church is a social ethic."[3] He and Willimon write: ". . . We want to argue that Christianity is mostly about politics — politics as defined by the gospel. . . . We argue that the political task of Christians is to be the church rather than transform the world."[4] The integrity of the biblical Jesus requires the integrity of an immigrant and alien Christian community in this world. While the approach of Yoder, Hauerwas, and Willimon may be commended for its earnest and saintly desire to emulate the earthly life-calling of our Lord in a community, critics point out that their ethic is grounded in an insufficient Christology that may be more appropriately termed "Jesuology."[5]

The "ethic of Jesus" is not a sufficient Christian ethic. If one canvasses Luke's Gospel for the biblical Jesus, a monistic "Jesuology" is sure to emerge. In his day Martin Luther responded to similar proposals for an ethic of Jesus: "If you wish to do just as Christ did, you will have to be born of a virgin, raise the dead, walk on water, take no wife,

---

1. Stanley Hauerwas and William H. Willimon would most probably protest my grouping them in Niebuhr's category of "Christ-against-culture"; however, their "discriminating modes for discerning how Christians should see the good and bad in 'culture'" leads to a radical ecclesiology warranting this classification. Cf. their *Resident Aliens: Life in the Christian Colony* (Nashville: Abingdon Press, 1989), 39-48.

2. Hauerwas and Willimon, *Resident Aliens,* 18.

3. Stanley Hauerwas, *The Peaceable Kingdom* (Notre Dame: University of Notre Dame Press, 1983), 99.

4. Hauerwas and Willimon, *Resident Aliens,* 30, 38.

5. For this insight I am indebted to my colleague Dr. Keith Pavlischek, director of the *Civitas* Forum at the Center for Public Justice in Annapolis, MD.

have no gold, nor any manservant or maidservant. . . . Christ was a preacher. . . . Do not take everything that Christ did as an example."[6] Luther makes a case for the special calling of Jesus in God's plan of redemption and warns against making the earthly example of our Lord normative for Christian ethics. Christian ethics must account for the diversity of callings that exist as a result of God's creation order. The cultural mandate of Genesis 1:28 is predicated upon God's design and purpose for various callings.

In surveying the totality of Christian revelation, especially John's Gospel or Paul's Letter to the Colossians, we find that the image of an eternal, pre-incarnate, pre-historical, cosmic Christ emerges to complement the incarnate and historical Jesus. It is Christ the King, the second person of the Trinity who with God the Father and God the Holy Spirit commissioned Adam and Eve to develop a flourishing culture. Therefore, the trinitarian Christ of Genesis 1 and John 1 must be harmonized with Jesus the Savior and Redeemer in the synoptic Gospels. Practically what this means for ethics is that an "ethic of Jesus" must be coupled with a creation ethic which takes into account Jesus' lordship over all of earthly existence and cultural life. Creation ordinances, natural law, moral norms woven into the warp and woof of the created universe must be included in a biblically trinitarian Christian ethic. As Niebuhr pointed out, "The knottiest theological problem raised by the Christ-against-culture movement is the problem of the relation of Jesus Christ to the Creator of nature and Governor of history. . . ."[7]

According to Niebuhr's construct, the second type of response to the enduring problem is "Christ-of-culture." This position recognizes "fundamental agreement between Christ and culture."[8] The person and work of Christ is harmonized with culture. Jesus is viewed as hero of society and champion of civilization, its progress and development. Therefore, tensions are minimized between the world and the church; between public law as an expression of moral

6. Martin Luther, *The Martin Luther Christmas Book,* trans. and ed. Roland H. Bainton (Philadelphia: Fortress Press, 1948), 35, 36.

7. H. Richard Niebuhr, *Christ and Culture* (New York: Harper and Row, 1951), 80.

8. Niebuhr, *Christ and Culture,* 41.

norms and the grace of the gospel; and between the socially "progressive" ethics of expressive individualism and the covenantally binding virtues of Christian character. From this vantage point the Christian faith must be made relevant to the culture by refashioning it to fit the constructs and categories of the prevailing worldview. Currently, within the Anglican Communion there is perhaps no more notorious representative of this approach than the Bishop of Newark, New Jersey, John Shelby Spong. His most recent book, *Why Christianity Must Change or Die,* argues for a postmodern pantheistic creed to replace the outmoded and premodern orthodox trinitarian theism of Chalcedon.[9] Spong views himself to be courageously fighting a rearguard action against the waning of Christianity in Europe and North America. He believes himself to be leading a missiological effort to make Christianity relevant to "the complex social and ethical issues of our day."[10] In the name of contextualization and inculturation Spong pleads for openness and innovation, not conservation. He calls on Anglicans to "embrace a new Reformation" lest our "great force in Western civilization sink into a negative and fearful position." But Spong's theological basis for this new Reformation is not the Christology of Martin Luther, the other Reformers, the Prayer Book, the Nicene Creed, or holy Scripture. A new Reformation demands a new theology because as Spong has recently written, "In the traditional Christian story, [former churchgoers] see a God who needed a blood offering of his son to save the fallen creation. Such a God has little appeal to these people's ears." Christ must be accommodated to the current culture.

Spong's Christ-of-culture, however, is not the biblical Christ. In fact, he is not Christ at all, but rather "a God presence" which premoderns called Christ[11] because they lacked "the tools to develop the elaborate Christologies that would mark the future."[12]

---

9. John Shelby Spong, *Why Christianity Must Change or Die: A Bishop Speaks to Believers in Exile* (San Francisco: Harper, 1998), 220-28.

10. John Shelby Spong, "Anglicans Get Literal," *The New York Times,* August 13, 1998.

11. Spong, *Why Christianity Must Change,* 221.

12. John Shelby Spong, *Resurrection Myth or Reality? A Bishop's Search for the Origins of Christianity* (San Francisco: Harper, 1994), 257.

Christ is not the "Lamb of God who takes away the sin of the world."[13] The necessity of substitutionary blood atonement is called into question as an outmoded narrative more appropriate to primitive peoples, but irrelevant and unfashionable to the ears of contemporary Westerners. What then does the memorial acclamation mean to Spong? "Christ has died" — the crucifixion is a cruel and unfortunate tragedy rather than a vicarious atonement to satisfy a just and holy God. "Christ is risen" — there is no resurrection, at least not really, not in space-time reality. Spong writes: "Angels who descend in earthquakes, speak, and roll back stones; tombs that are empty; apparitions that appear and disappear; rich men who make graves available; thieves who comment from their crosses of pain — these are legends all. Sacred legends, I might add, but legends nonetheless. . . . Jesus is alive in the heart of God."[14] In another of his books Spong writes, "Can we get beyond those biblical words to a place where we can touch the uninterpreted essence of Easter? Is the truth of Easter bound in time, or is it beyond time and therefore beyond history? . . . What meaning can the phrase 'He will come again to judge the living and the dead' have as the third millennium of the common era takes center stage? . . . Was that Gospel anticipation another example of inaccuracies in the biblical account?"[15]

Spong's own worldview is bifurcated. Intellectually, he is culturally captive to Enlightenment naturalism and therefore brings a so-called "scientific" and modernist anti-supernatural bias to holy Scripture. Religiously, however, Spong is a thoroughgoing postmodernist. The metanarrative of creation, fall, and redemption is cast aside for a syncretistic pantheism — a redemption-denying immanentism — which is tailor-made for our current philosophical climate of subjectivism. For Spong there is no biblical Christ. Indeed, there cannot be a biblical Christ because the biblical narrative is fanciful and unreliable. As a consequence, Spong's Christology might be more accurately identified as a "fill-in-the-blank-ology." Without an objective epistemic foundation it should be no surprise

13. John 1:29.
14. Spong, *Resurrection Myth,* 233, 257.
15. Spong, *Why Christianity Must Change,* 15-16.

that he writes, "I see no reason to believe that the people who participated in these councils of the church in that distant time were any more brilliant, insightful, or knowledgeable than are Christians of today. I do not, therefore, believe that the Christological formula was set for all time at Chalcedon in 451 C.E. I believe that we Christians must inevitably revisit Chalcedon and once again do the hard work of rethinking and redefining the Christ of experience for our time and in words and concepts appropriate to our world. I even favor the reopening of the debate between Arius and Athanasius on the nature of the Christ."[16] Spong's Christ-of-culture response sacrifices the integrity of a biblical Christ on the altar of cultural relevance. The new Christianity he champions is sub-Christian, even anti-Christian. Relevance is overcome by relativism and in the process the culture becomes irrelevant to the biblical Christ. Spong's Jesus is an experiential expression of a "God presence." The experience of the "now" as the operative mode for understanding life replaces a universally accessible, objective, and authoritative holy Scripture. The secondary authorities of mediated traditions, symbols, and rituals are readily deconstructed to conform to the experience of the "now." Even reason is held captive to the subjectivity of experience. In the end Richard Hooker's tri-legged stool of Scripture, tradition, and reason collapses to the banality of the now. In Spong's own words, "My business is to live now, to love now, and to be now. As I give my life, my love, and myself away now, I hope that others can be called into deeper life, greater love, fuller being, and that by expanding each other, we enter the infinity of what Paul Tillich called 'the eternal now.'"[17]

J. Gresham Machen's 1913 critique of nineteenth-century theological liberalism is as valid for Spong as it was for Friedrich Schleiermacher and Albrecht Ritschl. Machen wrote: ". . . Christianity may be subordinated to culture. That solution really, though to some extent unconsciously, is being favored by a very large and influential portion of the Church today. For the elimination of supernatural Christianity — so tremendously common today — really

16. Spong, *Why Christianity Must Change*, 19.
17. Spong, *Resurrection Myth*, 293.

makes Christianity merely natural. Christianity becomes a human product, a mere part of human culture. But as such it is something entirely different from the old Christianity that was based upon direct revelation from God. Deprived thus of its note of authority, the gospel is no gospel any longer; it is a cheque for untold millions — but without signature at the bottom. So in subordinating Christianity to culture we have destroyed Christianity, and what continues to bear the old name is a counterfeit."[18]

Between the two polarities of Christ-against-culture and Christ-of-culture are three options which compete for a *via media:* "Christ-above-culture," "Christ-and-culture in paradox," and "Christ the transformer of culture." It is within these last three categories of Niebuhr's that the currents of mainstream Anglicanism have flowed. The headwaters of these currents are found in St. Thomas, Luther, and St. Augustine and Calvin respectively. Furthermore, each of these three options is fully trinitarian in christological focus. And since all of these currents converge in the English Reformation, Anglicanism, I think, can rightfully lay claim to a large, theologically rich, and diverse body of thought on the relationship of Christ to culture.

For the sake of simplicity I would like to group these three options under a category which Machen used thirty-eight years prior to Niebuhr's construct — namely, "consecration." According to Machen the biblical Christ consecrates culture: "Instead of obliterating the distinction between the Kingdom and the world, or on the other hand withdrawing from the world into a sort of modernized intellectual monasticism, let us go forth joyfully, enthusiastically to make the world subject to God."[19] If I may be so bold as to suggest, the Anglican mainstream has always believed that Christ consecrates culture.

Within our own liturgical tradition there is an ancient Latin hymn which offers direction to the topic of the biblical Christ in a pagan culture. I refer to the text of *Te Deum laudamus.* Its authorship

18. J. Gresham Machen, "The Scientific Preparation of the Minister," *The Princeton Theological Review* XI (1913).

19. Machen, "The Scientific Preparation of the Minister."

is attributed to Ambrose (339-397), Bishop of Milan. Elements of the *Te Deum*, however, predate the bishop's authorship and can be traced back to the *Apostolic Constitutions* (c. 357).[20] Ambrose's formulation of the *Te Deum* occurs amid the christological controversies ranging from the Council of Nicea (325) to the Council of Chalcedon (451). In particular Ambrose found himself caught up in the Arian controversy with direct political pressure from Empress Justina to allow for Arian worship within his see. With Athanasian tenacity Ambrose resisted the Empress and maintained catholic orthodoxy during his episcopate. His exuberant hymn resounds with trinitarian orthodoxy — Father, Son and Holy Ghost. The text of *Te Deum* as it appears in the *Book of Common Prayer* is:

> We praise thee, O God; we acknowledge thee to be the Lord.
> All the earth doth worship thee, the Father everlasting.
> To thee all Angels cry aloud,
> the Heavens and all the Powers therein.
> To thee all Cherubim and Seraphim continually do cry:
> Holy, holy, holy Lord God of Sabaoth;
> Heaven and earth are full of the majesty of thy glory.
> The glorious company of the apostles praise thee.
> The goodly fellowship of the prophets praise thee.
> The noble army of the martyrs praise thee.
> The holy Church throughout all the world doth
>   acknowledge thee,
> the Father, of an infinite majesty,
> thine adorable, true, and only Son,
> also the Holy Ghost the Comforter.
>
> Thou art the King of glory, O Christ.
> Thou art the everlasting Son of the Father.
> When thou tookest upon thee to deliver man,
> thou didst humble thyself to be born of a Virgin.
> When thou hadst overcome the sharpness of death,
> thou didst open the kingdom of heaven to all believers.

20. Philip Schaff, *History of the Christian Church*, vol. III (New York: Charles Scribner's Sons, 1910), 591-93.

Thou sittest at the right hand of God, in the glory of the Father.
We believe that thou shalt come to be our judge.
We therefore pray thee, help thy servants,
whom thou hast redeemed with thy precious blood.
Make them to be numbered with thy saints,
in glory everlasting.

Of the thirty or so Ambrosian hymns, twelve are considered to be genuine, and of these, the *Te Deum* has proven to be by far the most celebrated and popular hymn.[21] This may be so because it accurately reflects the biblical and Nicene orthodoxy as well as religious piety of so many fourth and fifth-century believers. Yet these believers were still a minority throughout the Empire. Heresies had split the church and efforts of Christianizing an ancient pagan culture were ongoing. Even so, the triumphal hope and confidence of this hymn rings clear: "We praise thee, O God. . . . All the earth doth worship thee. . . . To thee all Angels cry aloud, the Heavens and all the Powers therein. . . ." The hymn exudes an undaunted optimism in the metaphysical reality that God exists and governs the universe, including affairs of humanity. The earthly and angelic realms of the created order attend to God's praise and glory. Think of this. In the midst of evil, oppression, civil strife, war, disease, pestilence, social and natural calamities, our early Christian fathers and mothers rejoiced in the fact that "Heaven and earth are full of the majesty of thy glory."

Even in the face of strident opposition and persecution (including death itself) the saints glorified God: "The noble army of the martyrs praise thee." The pagan Caesars could not command the ultimate allegiance of Christ's holy catholic and apostolic church. Emperor Diocletian's persecutions (305-311) were only a generation past and their horrors were indelibly impressed upon the memory of the saints. Grandfathers, grandmothers, aunts and uncles had died horribly for the public truth that Christ is king. This idea had powerfully explosive overtones for Roman political culture. Christ claimed totality for himself in Matthew's Gospel.[22] His lordship is irreconcilable with totalitarian tyranny.

21. Schaff, *History of the Christian Church*.
22. Matthew 28:18-20.

100

In this regard the *Te Deum* has been an inspirational hymn throughout the centuries during many such pressing trials and tribulations. Church historian Henri Daniel-Rops records that the *Te Deum* was sung during the French Revolution's Reign of Terror by the Ursuline nuns of Valenciennes who were awaiting their deaths and praying for their executioners' salvation.[23]

Crown and Cross

The biblical Christology of the *Te Deum* anticipates the Council of Chalcedon: ". . . our Lord Jesus Christ, the same perfect in Godhead and also perfect in manhood; truly God and truly man, of a reasonable soul and body; consubstantial with the Father according to the Godhead, and consubstantial with us according to the Manhood; in all things like unto us, without sin. . . ."[24] Balanced theological emphasis on the two natures of Christ is essential to a right ordering of the relationship between Christ and culture.

> Thou art the King of glory, O Christ.
> Thou art the everlasting Son of the Father.

The hymn's second verse opens with an orthodox Nicene Christology. The "King of glory" is the eternal Cosmic Creator-Christ. With respect to culture, two things should be said about Christ's two natures. First, Christ's divinity as Creator-King and Lawgiver is the ontological grounding for universal, transcontextual, transcultural, eternal absolutes. In this regard Christ transcends culture. He stands above it as its Creator and Sustainer. If Christ is the King of Glory, the Creator of an ordered universe, then we can have confidence that truth, goodness, and beauty objectively exist. Because they emanate from a perfect, omnipotent, and omniscient being, truth, goodness, and beauty are final, specific, and authoritative. Consequently, there

23. Henri Daniel-Rops, *The Church in an Age of Revolution 1789-1870* (London: J. M. Dent & Son, 1965), 36.

24. Philip Schaff, *The Creeds of Christendom*, vol. II: *The Latin and Greek Creeds* (1931; Grand Rapids: Baker Book House, 1985), 62.

ought to be no relativism, skepticism, or social construction about
them. Their accessibility and discovery, however, is problematic without God's self-disclosure in nature, Scripture, and finally in the incarnation of his Son. God's self-disclosing Word, living and written, is inevitably infallible, trustworthy, and true.

> When thou tookest upon thee to deliver man,
> thou didst humble thyself to be born of a Virgin.
> When thou hadst overcome the sharpness of death,
> thou didst open the kingdom of heaven to all believers.

Second, Christ's humanity dignifies the creation. If Christ's
Creator-Kingship universalizes truth, goodness, and beauty, then
the incarnation contextualizes these ideals in a particular time and
place. Jesus is not only "the everlasting Son of the Father," but also
the flesh and blood Son of Man in a specific time and place. As
Scripture records, Christ was "born of a woman, born under law, to
redeem those under law that we might receive the full rights of
sons."[25] Our Lord was born into a particular family, ethnicity, religious tradition, and culture. Through the incarnation the transcendent Christ was made immanent in a historical time and local place.
In the incarnation the universals and the particulars are brought
into congruence. Through the divine incarnation human life and a
humane way of life were sanctified. The presence and participation
of the God-man sanctified the ordinary, commonplace, everyday activities of human life. Our Lord labored as a carpenter, prepared and
ate meals, slept, conversed at the marketplace and in the taverns, at-
tended synagogue and temple worship and instruction, visited wedding feasts, witnessed baptisms, and even paid taxes. The God-man
Jesus participated in the life of local culture and in doing so redirected it toward its Maker, his heavenly Father.

It is the "sharpness of death" which opens the way for a hell-
bent culture to be redirected toward the "kingdom of heaven." Jesus
the Redeemer and Savior, to whom the "whole creation" looks for
liberation "from its bondage to decay,"[26] is the Lamb of God who

25. Galatians 4:4, 5.
26. Romans 8:21, 22.

102

takes away the sin of the world by the propitiation of his sacrificial death on the cross. Access to "the Father everlasting" is made possible through the vicarious blood atonement of his Son. It is because of this real space-time event that all believers can stand with "the glorious company of the apostles," "the goodly fellowship of the prophets," and "the noble army of the martyrs" in the worship of God.

> Thou sittest at the right hand of God, in the glory
> of the Father.
> We believe that thou shalt come to be our judge.

Not only is Christ incarnate, but he is risen from the dead and ascended. The resurrection was a physical reality that occurred in space and time. Easter and Ascension Day mark our liturgical calendar with good reason. These real events confirm the cosmic totality of Christ's lordship over all. Our celebrations of these two days affirm the reality that sin and death is conquered, humanity is restored, cultural life is renewed, creation is re-created. Though today we benefit from this metaphysical reality only in part, we anxiously await Christ's return for its fulfillment — the restoration of all things.

> We therefore pray thee, help thy servants. . . .

What do Jesus' crown and cross mean for us today? When we recite the *Te Deum*, how does it challenge us to struggle with the relationship of Christ and culture? I think that the *Te Deum* is an appropriate rubric for exploring Niebuhr's enduring problem as it relates to our own cultural context. Whereas the monist "Jesuology" of Yoder, Hauerwas, and Willimon isolates the church from the culture, and the pantheistic "fill-in-the-blank-ology" of Spong capitulates to the culture's zeitgeist; the biblical Christology of the *Te Deum laudamus* provides the theological parameters for constructing an Anglican *via media* to responsible engagement with pagan culture. Christ consecrates culture.

The Norm of Culture and the Cultural Norm

In the biblical narrative, culture is part of what Calvin called the "order of Creation."[27] Culture is a norm of creation arising from God's creative activity. It is particularly that aspect of God's creative work which he shares with humanity. God, in fact, mandated the development of culture in the very first chapter of Genesis: "Be fruitful and increase in number; fill the earth and subdue it. Rule over the fish of the sea and the birds of the air and over every living creature that moves on the ground."[28] The first Adam and his bride, Eve, were commissioned by God to procreate — to raise and nurture children. Secondly, and as a natural realization of this first task, they had a cultural task. The Garden of Eden was to be tilled and cultivated. Paradise was to be developed into a flourishing civilization, a City of and for God. The *telos* of humanity is a *polis*.[29]

This idea of *telos* or purpose is essential to understanding culture in Christian perspective. Missionary apologist Lesslie Newbigin insightfully has observed that the elimination of purpose as an investigative question has been an unintended consequence of the scientific revolution. Concentration on cause-and-effect relations is the focus of scientific method and in this process an orientation on function has eclipsed questions about end, purpose, or design.[30] A preoccupation with the "How?" not the "Why?" questions has depersonalized and even mechanized the universe. The cosmic and human story of creation is lost. As a consequence nature becomes something to be conquered. Whereas the biblical writers and other ancients viewed culture as in fundamental congruence with and arising from nature, moderns pursue culture as something to be imposed on nature. The modern view is that reality, or the nature of

27. John Calvin, *Institutes,* I.xiv.22.

28. Genesis 1:28.

29. For a very thorough development of this theme see Oliver O'Donovan, *The Desire of Nations: Rediscovering the Roots of Political Theology* (Cambridge: Cambridge University Press, 1997).

30. Lesslie Newbigin, *The Gospel in a Pluralist Society* (Grand Rapids: Eerdmans, 1989), 16, 36.

things, is something from which to be liberated. Freedom is juxtaposed with nature.

However, from a Christian creational perspective nature is something in which we participate. Christ's incarnation leads us to develop a christological ontology or a christocentric view of reality. What is a Christian view of reality or being? What does Christ's incarnation and participation in the creation mean for culture? The language of Chalcedon drives us to these questions. Words and phrases like "perfect in manhood," "reasonable soul and body," "consubstantial with us according to manhood," etc. invite questions about the nature of things and coincidental questions about ethics. What is the nature of freedom? Can freedom be reconciled with order? What does freedom have to do with limitation, especially the natural limitations of time, place, body, gender, etc.?

In his classic essay on moral education, *The Abolition of Man*, C. S. Lewis argues for the objectivity of values. According to Lewis, the idea of objective right and wrong is grounded in the way things are, the nature of things or reality. Therefore, the question of moral education is how to conform the soul to creational reality, the nature of things, or natural law. With the ancients, Lewis argues that the ordering of affections occurs through acquiring knowledge of the law, practicing self-discipline, and cultivating the virtues.[31] Since culture arises from God's creative activity and is an aspect of creation that he shares with humanity, culture is to be ordered so as to fit the created reality. Therefore, education, as a function of culture, is to direct the soul with the "grain of the universe" and not against it. This is as true for the "sciences" as it is for the humanities.

If we can infer from the biblical narrative that the *telos* of humanity is a *polis*, then it is appropriate to ask, what is the means to this end? In the cultural mandate the family is the central means to the end. God's commission was given to humanity through our covenantal parents, Adam and Eve. The family as instituted by God, then, is the fulcrum of civilization. It is the link between nature and culture. There is a direct and foundational correlation between fam-

31. C. S. Lewis, *The Abolition of Man* (1944; New York: Touchstone, 1996), 17-37.

ily and social order. The Dutch statesman and Reformed theologian Abraham Kuyper wrote that in the order of creation "political life, in its entirety, would have evolved itself . . . from the life of the family." Yet even after the cosmic consequences of the fall, Kuyper argues that "marriage remains the foundation of human society and the family retains its position as the primordial sphere in sociology."[32] The symbiotic duality of male and female sexes forms the basis for marriage and family life. The metaphysics of human sexuality include the innate power of biological reproduction that is structured by God to be love-giving and life-promoting. In procreation, children are born who are naturally and organically interrelated to parents and siblings. This creation order forms the basis for the interrelatedness, interconnectedness, and interdependence of human society. Roman Catholic teaching also emphasizes the organic relation of family to culture: "'Since the Creator of all things has established the conjugal partnership as the beginning and basis of human society,' the family is 'the first and vital cell of society.' The family has vital and organic links with society, since it is its foundation and nourishes it continually through its role of service to life. . . ."[33] In a biblical cosmology, the idea that family fosters culture is a cultural norm.

The paganization of culture occurs very early in the biblical narrative. Adam and Eve's disobedience to God's explicit command recorded in the third chapter of Genesis radically affects nature, the norm of culture, and the cultural norm. As a consequence of their moral choice, sin counteracts God's order of creation. Evil and death corrupt nature. Cosmically, things begin to fall apart. Correspondingly, the naturally directed trajectory of family and culture toward the City of God is skewed. Nature, family, and culture are insufficient and unable to guide and direct human life toward its God-ordained destiny.

One profoundly grave tragedy of the fall is family brokenness.

32. Abraham Kuyper, *Lectures on Calvinism* (1931; Grand Rapids: Eerdmans, 1987), 80, 91.

33. John Paul II, *Familiaris Consortio* (Boston: Pauline Books & Media, 1981), 67, 68. The Pope cites the Second Vatican Ecumenical Council, Decree on the Apostolate of the Laity, *Apostolicam Actuositatem*, n. 11.

This moral reality is made poignantly evident in the first murder. A mis-ordering of affections results in pain and death. The right ordering of affections is: Love God and love your neighbor as yourself. Unfortunately Cain's alienation from God seeds jealousy in his heart that germinates in murder. When Cain kills his brother Abel, family dysfunction is manifested in the horror of spilt blood. Spiritual kinship as well as flesh and blood kinship were violated in the natural order of things. This event is so disruptive to the creation order that Scripture records that Abel's "blood cries out to Me [God] from the ground."[34] Cain's murder of his brother ultimately stemmed from idolatry. Abel's death was the first ritualistic murder in the pagan cult of self-worship. Creation order, the natural law teaches that we are our "brother's keeper." Indeed, family and cultural life is predicated upon this fact.

The mis-ordering of affections in creation's first family ultimately led to the demise of antediluvian civilization and to the dysfunction of culture right down to the present day. Narcissism is antifamily and anticultural. Narcissistic culture is an oxymoron. The religious origins of contemporary idolatrous notions of the "un-encumbered self" are to be found in Genesis. The health, well-being, and right ordering of affections is critical to the commonwealth. Pathology in the family leads to pathology in society.

Plato rightly, if incompletely, argued that the substance of politics is the *psyche* or soul. For Plato, the *polis* or city was the soul written at large. The science of politics was predicated upon anthropology or the study of the nature of humanity. Disorder of the soul leads to social disorder. Unfortunately, Plato's individualist-statist assumptions undervalue the role of the family. For if the family constitutes irreducible social reality, then the substance of politics is the family. Due to the interrelatedness, interconnectedness, and interdependence of human society, the effects of family disorder can be multiplied exponentially. The well-ordered soul in the social context of a well-ordered family is the key to vibrant culture and commonwealth.

Right now in the United States our national conversation is

34. Genesis 4:10.

107

preoccupied with the pathology and dysfunction in the American First Family. In our country there is an ongoing spirited public discourse and debate about the relationship between public and private spheres of life. People are asking themselves and others whether private behavior between "consenting adults" has any relevance to public life. If there is any value in such a national conversation, I personally hope that it will lead people to reconsider some political first principles of the creation order. A first principle for consideration in American political culture is: Does the unencumbered self or does the covenantally-bonded family define irreducible social reality?

Restoration of the Norm of Culture and the Cultural Norm

If the paganization of culture occurs very early in the biblical narrative, so does the promise of Christ and the hope of Christianizing culture. The proto-evangel of Genesis 3:15 speaks of a future "offspring" of Eve, a descendent who will "crush" the head of the evil serpent. A second Adam will redeem creation from sin's curse. The church, the bride of the second Adam, is given a "Great Commission" to spread the gospel of life in Christ around the world. The good news is that the sacrificial death and resurrection of God's incarnate son have repaired the trajectory toward the City of God. A reconciled humanity in its family and cultural dimensions can be restored to wellness and wholeness. At the end of the age the "kingdom of this world has become the kingdom of our Lord and of his Christ."[35] In this world persons from "every tribe and language and people and nation"[36] constitute "the Holy City, the new Jerusalem, coming down out of heaven prepared as a bride beautifully dressed for her husband."[37]

It is important to point out that this cosmic and human story

35. Revelation 11:15.
36. Revelation 5:9.
37. Revelation 21:2.

of redemption is told using the language of marriage and family. Salvation history employs the ideas of God as husband and Israel as an adulterous wife in the Old Testament. In the New Testament God is Father, Jesus is Son, Mary is mother of the God-man whom she vaginally delivers into this world, the church is the bride of Christ, believers are brothers and sisters, children of God, coheirs with the Son. Marriage figures prominently in holy Scripture. Genesis begins with Adam and Eve's marriage. Jesus performs his first miracle at a wedding ceremony. History is consummated with a wedding feast of Christ and his bride, the church, in the Revelation. Marriage and family as a motif of redemption points to the centrality and prominence of this institution in nature and Scripture. Confusion about the creational norm of this institution contributes to rendering the gospel unintelligible. In light of the recent Lambeth Conference resolution on sexuality, there is much more at stake than traditional Christian sexual ethics. For if the church were to waver on the nature and teleology of marriage and family, it would contribute to making the story of redemption incomprehensible.

Augustine grasped the importance of the family as a natural window to the eternal realities. In this regard the importance of the family transcends its centrality to cultural life and the commonwealth. The meaning and significance of family is more than penultimate. The family is more than "the first and vital cell of society" or "the primordial sphere of sociology." Ultimately, the family is a "school of virtue." For in the family God is at work in us to shape, mold, and fashion us in the eternal virtue of love. As St. John writes, "For anyone who does not love his brother, whom he has seen, cannot love God, whom he has not seen."[38] According to Augustine, Christians should not regret this passage of time "for in it they are schooled for eternity."[39]

It was the hope of the Eternal City that animated St. Augustine to consider what the biblical Christ in a pagan culture meant for Christians of his day. During Augustine's life classical civilization was breathing its last; a Dark Age was impending. In 410 the unthinkable

38. 1 John 4:20.
39. Augustine, *City of God*, I, 29.

had happened. Alaric, King of the Visigoths, sacked the Imperial City. Rome's security had been compromised for the first time in eight centuries. By 476 a barbarian would rule Rome and classical culture would be surrendered to a dark cultural barbarism. Augustine lived between two worlds: classical antiquity and medieval Christendom. The Christianization of the classical world had been underway since the first century. The gospel proclaimed by the Apostles eventually produced a largely theonomous culture which resulted in a Constantinian theocracy by 325. Even so, this culture retained many pagan elements. Augustine wrote the *City of God* in response to a sizable pagan minority within the empire who charged that Rome fell because of the empire's abandonment of the old pagan religions. Augustine's work holds forth a high ecclesiology of the visible church as a sojourning and pilgrim element of the Eternal City in this world. Though the city of this world (classical civilization in Augustine's circumstance) passes away, the Eternal City endures forever. With this hope and confidence the church proceeded to engage the onslaught of pagan culture. As the gospel went forth in Europe to change lives and a pagan culture's way of life, the church's ecclesiastical organization and visible identification with the kingdom of God led to the reorganization of society. Christendom emerged in the Middle Ages.

One particular story of relevance to us is the conversion of the pagan King Edwin of Northumbria in 627 as recounted by the Venerable Bede in his *History of the English Church and People*. Through the Christian influence of his family, especially his wife Ethelberga, and the evangelistic persistence of Paulinus, Bishop of Northumbria, the king had been moved to faith in Christ. Pope Boniface had even sent a warm pastoral exhortation to the queen urging her to use the experience of her own conversion as "an opportunity to kindle a spark of the true religion in your husband, for in this way He [God] will more swiftly inspire not only the mind of your illustrious Consort to love of Him, but the minds of his subjects as well. . . . Let it therefore be your constant prayer that God of His mercy will bless and enlighten the King, so that you, who are united in earthly marriage, may after this life remain united for ever in the bond of faith. My illustrious daughter, persevere in using every effort to soften his heart by teaching him the laws of God. Help him to understand the excellence of the mystery, which you have accepted and believe, and the wonderful reward that you have been accounted worthy to receive in this new birth. Melt the coldness of his heart by teaching him about the Holy Spirit, so that the warmth of divine faith may enlighten his mind through your constant encouragement, and remove the chilling and ruinous errors of paganism. . . ."[40]

Because of the Christian witness of his family and pastor, King Edwin "was both willing and obliged to accept the Faith which he was taught, but said that he must discuss the matter with his principal advisers and friends." Subsequently, he assembled the High Priest, Coifi, and other trusted counselors to ascertain their opinion on the matter. Coifi opens the discussion, "Your Majesty, let us give careful consideration to this new teaching, for I frankly admit that, in my experience, the religion that we have hitherto professed seems valueless and powerless. . . . Therefore, if on examination these new teachings are found to be better and more effectual, let us not hesitate to accept them." Lamenting their pagan religion's lack of certainty of knowledge for understanding life another adviser counsels the king, "Therefore if this new teaching can reveal any more certain knowledge, it seems only right that we should follow it." Bede records that the remaining counselors gave the same advice.

The pagan culture of Northumbria was crying out for a religion that offered effective and certain knowledge. They sought a cult for the development of a culture. Hungering for a way of life that was more "effectual" and "certain" in its correspondence to reality or the way things are, the pagans of Northumbria wanted the surety of truth. After hearing Bishop Paulinus's biblical story of a beautiful creation fallen and corrupted by sin, yet redeemed by a Savior from "the Devil's enslaving tyranny," the High Priest was convinced. Coifi confesses, "I have long realized that there is nothing in what we worshiped, for the more diligently I sought after truth in our religion, the less I found. I now publicly confess that this teaching clearly reveals truths that will afford us the blessings of life, salvation, and eternal happiness."[41] Upon reception of the

40. Bede, *History of the English Church and People*, II, 11.
41. Bede, *History*, II, 13.

Christian faith Northumbria enjoyed civil peace and prosperity. The fruit of the gospel was made manifest in a transformed culture.

The lesson is that bad ideas can bear the weight of reality for only so long. As an extension of human nature, a culture is like a human body. It seeks its own health and wellness. A vibrant culture cannot be built on a cult of lies and death. Sooner or later it will become gravely ill and may even die. On the other hand, a cult of "the truth and the life" fosters the development of a culture that affirms the same. The pagan culture of Northumbria in the early seventh century was intellectually and spiritually exhausted. The bad ideas of its religious cult could no longer bear the weight of reality. Christianity was embraced because it was powerfully true — true because its cosmic and human story squared with reality, its logic and mystery. The Christian faith now appropriated by the people of Northumbria, including its ruling elite, was made incarnate in their culture.

The Biblical Christ in Our Pagan Culture

As early as 1939, T. S. Eliot pondered whether or not Western history had reached a point at which "practising Christians must be recognized as a minority (whether static or diminishing) in a society which had ceased to be Christian." Eliot surmised that Christians faced a crossroads in the scope of Western history: "I believe that the choice before us is between the formation of a new Christian culture, and the acceptance of a pagan one."[42] In 1960, Christopher Dawson, a Roman Catholic contemporary of Eliot, observed, "It seems clear that the present state of the post-Christian world, a world which is no longer Christian but which retains a vague sympathy for or sentimental attachment to Christian moral ideals, is essentially a temporary one. Unless there is a revival or restoration of Christian culture — of the social life of the Christian community — modern civilization will become secularist in a more

42. T. S. Eliot, *Christianity and Culture* (1939; San Diego: Harcourt Brace & Company, 1978), 9, 10.

positive and aggressive way than it is today."[43] Both of these Christian thinkers possessed a sober realization that Western culture had undergone a major transformation in its organizing beliefs, ideals, and values. In their assessment the culture was "post-Christian" rather than positively pagan. What would be their assessment of Western culture today?

It seems to me that it is now more appropriate to speak of our culture as pagan rather than post-Christian. The Christian understanding of transcendence, truth, and tradition is under direct assault from the two main currents of the contemporary zeitgeist: postmodernism and modernity. By the term "postmodernism" I mean the spiritual/intellectual movement of philosophical deconstruction which can be more simply defined as an "incredulity toward metanarratives."[44] In my use of the term "modernity" I do not refer to modernism as a philosophical movement associated with the Enlightenment, but rather I use the term to describe the sociological trend of modernization. Modernity is a movement of technological development and innovation that has altered social structures and institutions and ways in which they mediate culture and reality.

Postmodernism is a direct assault on Christianity because of its "incredulity" toward the grand narrative of holy Scripture and ensuing texts like the Creeds, Prayer Book, etc. Its rejection of the objectivity of truth, the idea that truth corresponds to a reality that is "out there," leads to a skepticism about the Christian grand narrative of creation, fall, and redemption. Likewise all doctrinal formulations like the Nicene Creed which claim to describe an objective reality are also subject to a postmodern culture of disbelief. Postmodernism's skepticism goes beyond perennial issues in epistemology and is grounded in a new ontology. Whereas Christianity and the Enlightenment posited a universe, cosmology, or worldview and thus universal truth, postmodernism abandons a universe, uni-

43. Christopher Dawson, *The Historic Reality of Christian Culture* (London: Routledge and Kegan Paul, 1960), 41, 42.
44. Jean-François Lyotard, *The Postmodern Condition: A Report on Knowledge*, trans. Geoff Bennington and Brian Massumi (Minneapolis: University of Minnesota Press, 1984), xxiii, xxiv.

versal whole, or ultimate reality. Postmodernism has no worldview but only linguistically created worlds of conflicting interpretations. In postmodernism's anti-worldview there can be no God, Maker of heaven and earth. Without ultimate reality and truth there is no final criterion. In this case, as C. S. Lewis reminded us, "Unless the measuring rod is independent of the thing measured, we can do no measuring."[45] All interpretations are equally valid and invalid. Though pragmatic utility may lend some credence to an interpretation, there is no objective standard for evaluation. Thus there are only conflicting interpretations of linguistically created worlds which vie for ascendancy in a struggle for power.

At its core postmodernism is animated by a "gnostic impulse," as Roger Lundin has keenly observed. Because grace is not to be found in this world, the self must be detached from the traditions of the past, the communities of the present, and the mysteries of creational life.[46] "[E]mbeddedness of the self within the limits of nature and the constrictions of society" is the great evil according to these contemporary gnostics.[47] The new gnostic gospel is "the gospel of language; its saving message is that language does not lead us to any secret truths or havens of beauty and power but rather is itself the only place of safety and delight in a hostile world. In contemporary theory, the ironic, playful consolations of language are the postmodern equivalent of a gnostic heaven in which weary souls may find rest."[48] In the new gnosticism transcendence and truth are replaced by subjective perspectivism and unending "conversation." Without an ultimate reality and universal rationality tradition must yield to progress. Thus perspective, parsing, and "progress" replace transcendence, truth, and tradition.

Without transcendence, truth, and tradition, Pandora's box is open to new faiths, especially those that draw on strains of ancient and primitive paganism. The Eastern religions, the New Age move-

45. C. S. Lewis, *Christian Reflections* (1967; Grand Rapids: Eerdmans, 1992), 73.

46. Roger Lundin, *The Culture of Interpretation: Christian Faith and the Postmodern World* (Grand Rapids: Eerdmans, 1993), 78-103.

47. Lundin, *The Culture of Interpretation*, 81.

48. Lundin, *The Culture of Interpretation*, 89.

ment, and environmentalism are especially compatible with postmodernism. As deconstructionists parse every word, dissect every sentence, redact every paragraph, decompose every narrative and consequently every truth claim, they assault form in the name of freedom. Set free from the constraints of an external world with its objectivist and rational categories, the individual can be mystically reconciled with nature and culture. The divine self is the religious promise of postmodernism. The temptation to be creator of one's universe is a very ancient one. In fact, it is an intellectually fashionable refashioning of the old Serpent's promise to Eve in the Garden of Eden, "You will be like God. . . ."[49]

The biblical Christ in our pagan postmodern culture affirms the credulity of the metanarrative. Christ is the Alpha and Omega, the beginning and the end of the grand narrative of creation, fall, and redemption. Furthermore, he is the center of the story. Notwithstanding postmodernism's decry of the loss of a "center" and disparagement of "logocentrism,"[50] Christ is the Divine *Logos*. In spite of spiritual and intellectual opposition to this onto-Christology, as Dietrich Bonhoeffer reminds us, "We must continue to emphasize that Christ is truly the centre of human existence, the centre of history and now also the centre of nature. . . . The mediator as fulfiller of the law and liberator of creation is all this for the whole of human existence."[51]

In 627 the pagans of Northumbria rejected their gods because they were insufficient. The biblical Christ offered them "effectual" and "certain knowledge" about this life and the afterlife. These pagans of the seventh century longed for truth. They desired to know the permanent things upon which better family and cultural life might be constructed. The High Priest Coifi's confession was that Christianity "reveals truth that will afford us the blessings of life, salvation and eternal happiness." In many ways their cultural life is analogous to our own. As postmodern culture more closely resem-

---

49. Genesis 3:5.

50. Jacques Derrida, *Of Grammatology*, trans. Gayatri Chakravorky Spivak (Baltimore: Johns Hopkins University Press, 1976).

51. Dietrich Bonhoeffer, *Christ the Center*, trans. Edward H. Robertson (1960; San Francisco: HarperCollins, 1978), 65.

bles the pagan spirituality of Northumbria, we can have confidence that the ideals, beliefs, and values of Christianity are true and compellingly so. Just as paganism in Northumbria was spiritually and intellectually inadequate and therefore wanting, we can be assured that postmodernism is so today. As a religion, postmodernism may be fashionable among the priestly class of academics, but it falls short of fostering and ordering a way of life that is in harmony with reality. Postmodern priests of the New Age religions, Eastern mysticism, and environmentalism, like Coifi of old, may diligently propose their faiths, but daily life can neither square well nor fare well on deconstructionist assumptions about reality. Our culture, its peoples and families are hungering for the truth.

Though postmodernism's "incredulity toward metanarratives" is a direct assault on Christianity, I do not believe postmodernism is the greatest challenge for the church in our pagan culture. Modernity, the second current of the contemporary zeitgeist, poses a more pressing summons for the meaning of a biblical Christ in a pagan culture. The fact that modernity is not a direct assault on the faith is precisely why it is so threatening. There is danger in its subtlety. In many Christian circles, the affront of modernity is not even perceived. To the contrary, modernity is more often readily embraced, though unwittingly, by the theologically orthodox. Within the Anglican Communion, while liberals are tempted to subordinate Christ to postmodernism, many evangelicals eagerly receive modernization as an opportunity to advance worldwide evangelism. In doing so they may be making a Faustian bargain with the devil of modernity.[52] Dr. Os Guinness, an Anglican and sociologist, observes, "World-denying conservatism has become virtually impossible. And Christendom's ultimate worldling today is not the Christian liberal but the Christian conservative. . . . In its sweatless, disincarnate, electric form, modern evangelism has created the ultimate parody of the incarnation."[53]

52. I am indebted to Dr. Os Guinness of the Trinity Forum in Burke, Virginia, for the benefit of his thinking on modernity.
53. Os Guinness, *Mission Modernity: Seven Checkpoints in the Modern World* (Burke, VA: The Trinity Forum, 1996), 2.

How does modernity threaten the integrity and character of the gospel and the church? How can technology, especially mass media and computer-telecommunications technology, compromise the Divine *Logos*? These questions are directly relevant for day-to-day family and parish life.

Modernity's benefits are innumerable. No one can seriously deny the great advantages science and technology bestow upon human life and civilization. Household appliances like dishwashers, coffeemakers, and microwave ovens; lifesaving and life-extending medicines and health care facilities; the personal computer with its fingertip access to the information superhighway; instantaneous worldwide cellular telephone communications; relatively safe and speedy automobile and air travel; electronic banking, ATMs, and credit cards, etc. have all made living in this century unparalleled to living at any other time in history. Modernity offers us the first universal or global civilization since the Tower of Babel. Like the ancient tower's architects, modernity promises a limitless horizon.

However, the price exacted for such a universal civilization is the loss of particular or local culture, even the family. Modernity is anticultural. Its universalizing tendencies run counter to the particularities of culture. Culture arises out of nature through the mediation of the family. The family is the link between nature and culture. As an outgrowth of nature, culture is connected with nature through the biological, social, and historical bonds of family life. Family cultivates culture. As Eliot writes, "The primary channel of transmission of culture is the family: no man wholly escapes from the kind, or wholly surpasses the degree, of culture which he acquired from his early environment. . . . But when I speak of the family, I have in mind a bond which embraces . . . a piety towards the dead, however obscure, and a solicitude for the unborn, however remote."[54]

Arising from nature through the family, culture, therefore, has an affinity with nature. Culture's end or purpose is to be in harmony with nature and God. The answer to the Westminster Shorter Catechism's first question says as much, "Man's chief end is to glo-

54. Eliot, *Christianity and Culture*, 115, 116.

rify God and to enjoy him forever."[55] The Christian faith affirms the ultimate harmony of nature and culture with God in Christ. We have already examined the prominence of family in salvation history, but consider some other "this world" affirming images: believers are salt, light, wheat, and branches; the church is a rock, living stones, and body; the kingdom of God is a landowner, sower, mustard seed, yeast, material treasure, dragnet, etc. Nature has a sacramental cast. Creation and life have a positive richness that is derived from God. Nature is designed to reflect the Divine Nature. Culture is commissioned to lead and direct us from nature to God. Nature, culture, and God find harmony in the incarnate Christ.

Culture is communal and its community arises from the organic bonds of family life. In culture the social bonds of tradition, ritual, and symbol are joined to the organic bonds of family. Traditions, rituals, and symbols bind a people beyond the natural affinities of blood kinship. Culture moves us by its traditions, rituals, and symbols to see a transcendent reality mirrored in nature, yet beyond and above nature. Tradition, ritual, and symbol fire the collective imagination of the community for the spiritual and intellectual apprehension of God in his truth, goodness, and beauty.

Modernity, on the other hand, seeks to subjugate nature, to harness it, to overcome it, to transcend its limitations of time, place, family, and body. From the Tower of Babel to the new electronic millennium of cyberspace, modernity has promised the heavens. But the way to the heavenlies is not a bodily earthly pilgrimage. The *via moderna* is not the way of the cross. Modernity's technological impetus for emancipation from the constraints of nature, culture, and tradition is fueled by the gnostic desire to be free from the embeddedness of earthly life. In contrast to a natural way of living in family and community, the way of modernity is new, contemporary, up-to-date, relevant, significant, spontaneous, instant, fast, clean, sleek, state of the art, simple, smart, no-nonsense, convenient, easy to use, happy, user friendly, customer oriented, risk-free with satisfaction guaranteed or your money back. Modernity offers us everything except culture.

55. Schaff, *History of the Christian Church,* vol. III, p. 676.

Modernity assails the family and community in scores of ways. Global and national economies uproot families from place, parents, grandparents, and graveyards. Furthermore, working requirements remove fathers and mothers from the home sometimes for extended periods of days, even weeks. Institutionalized daycare and compulsory education have led to what the late Christopher Lasch called the "socialization of reproduction" and the "proletarianization of parenthood." In this process the "helping professions" displace the natural roles of parents and grandparents.[56] The school bus carries students away from local neighborhoods to consolidated schools. The automobile encourages "commuters" to work, window shop, and worship at greater distances beyond the borders of their local communities. Satellite television, the personal computer, and Internet bring the world into our homes in such a way that many of us are more at home living in "virtual reality" than reality. As modernity makes the world our neighbor we become more concerned about television character Jerry Seinfeld's dating life than the impending divorce of our neighbors next door.

Modernity is individualistic and thus alienating and dehumanizing. Its tools of technology are not made to serve culture but to subjugate it.[57] They are designed to liberate the individual from the natural limitations of place, time, family, and body. But these very natural limitations lead us to communal and cultural life. Culture arises from the organic bonds of family in a natural habitat. Modernity shortcuts nature and as a consequence destroys or at least damages culture. The social bonds of cultural life are weakened. Tradition, ritual, and symbol are displaced, even forgotten. God is not seen. Modernity's civilization is a sanitized, pasteurized, and homogenized "world without windows" inhabited by "atheists unaware." Modernity's most devastating cultural effect is what Peter Berger calls the "secularization of consciousness."[58]

Suffice it to say that the *via moderna* is not the Anglican *via me-*

56. Christopher Lasch, *Haven in a Heartless World: The Family Besieged* (New York: Norton, 1977), 12-21.

57. See Neil Postman, *Technopoly: The Surrender of Culture to Technology* (New York: Vintage Books, 1992).

58. Peter Berger, *A Rumor of Angels* (New York: Doubleday, 1992).

dia. How is a biblical Christ in our pagan culture made manifest? What is the call of Nicene orthodoxy for this time and place? What must we do to heed Eliot's call for the formation of a new Christian culture?

Again the Venerable Bede's account of the 627 conversion of the pagans in Northumbria is instructive. There is an interesting passage in Pope Boniface's letter to Queen Ethelberga regarding her spiritual obligation to press for her husband's conversion "to the knowledge of the most high and undivided Trinity." The Pope writes:

> Our paternal responsibility moves us to urge Your Christian Majesty under God's guidance not to avoid the duty always imposed on us, in order that, with the assistance and strength of our Lord and Saviour Jesus Christ, the King may be added to the Christian fold. Only in this way will you enjoy the full privileges of marriage in perfect union, for the Scripture says, "The two shall become one flesh." But how can it be called a true union between you, so long as he remains alienated from your glorious Faith by the barrier of dark and lamentable error? Let it therefore be your constant prayer that God of His mercy will bless and enlighten the King, so that you, who are united in earthly marriage, may after this life remain united for ever in the bond of faith.

Boniface's strategy for the evangelization of Northumbria is directed to Northumbria's first family. Knowing that "our loving Redeemer has offered a saving remedy to the human race," the Pope encourages the queen to look forward to enjoying "the full privileges of marriage in perfect union." What the gospel means to the queen, king, and all of Northumbria is restoration and wholeness of family and cultural life as it should be, as it was originally supposed to be. The bond of "earthly marriage" mirrors the eternal unity in the "bond of faith." Starting with marriage, pagan culture would be transformed by the gospel. Expectant that the gospel would transform the king and his marriage, he concludes his letter, "And when we see the glory of God's redemption spreading ever more widely among you, we shall give glad and heartfelt thanks to God."

The active ministry of a pastor and parish supported the Christian witness of the queen. Justus, Archbishop of Canterbury, had consecrated Bishop Paulinus, in 625. Bede records, "Therefore, directly he entered the province he began to toil unceasingly with God's help not only to maintain the faith of his companions unimpaired, but if possible to bring some of the heathen to grace and faith by his teaching." In that year the queen gave birth to a daughter, Eanfeld, whom Paulinus baptized with twelve others, the first Northumbrians to receive Baptism. The king was profoundly moved by the miracle of life demonstrated in his new daughter and Paulinus's witness that "it was Christ who had given the queen a safe and painless delivery in response to his prayers."[59]

King Edwin was eventually converted to the faith and with him, the entire kingdom. Evangelism began in his home through the witness of a faithful spouse in the day-to-day activities of life. Additionally, the queen's pastor was faithful in his ministry of Word and sacrament. At a key moment in the life of the first family, the birth of their daughter, the king was spiritually moved yet closer to faith in Christ. Family and parish, spouse and priest were present in the life of Edwin. The incarnational ministries of Ethelberga and Paulinus led to the conversion of king and kingdom. It is a great story. The story may be ours to reenact. Let us hope so.

The Case for Catholic Parochialism

The biblical Christ in our pagan culture will only be made manifest in his people — the church. Intentional Christian community of families surrounding the Word and sacraments is the only way to form a Christian culture. Worship that is centered on the meta-narrative of the Divine Logos, coupled with a discipleship in family life that defies the dehumanizing influences of modernity, must be our response to the contemporary zeitgeist.

The local parish must be established as a center of life in the twenty-first century. In this regard, it ought to house both sanctuary and school. The parish is the church's first and most vital cell.

59. Bede, *History*, II, 9-11.

With the impending new dark ages the parish must conserve what remains of Christian culture, its Scripture, worship, learning, music, and art. As Niebuhr reminds us, "Let education and training lapse for one generation, and the whole grand structure of past achievements falls into ruin."[60] There is no doubt that the content and conduits of universal secular public education have substantially contributed to the secularization, even paganization of culture. Yet the increasing public visibility of Christian schooling and home schooling is indicative of the desire of Christian parents to provide a learning experience with an integrated Christian vision of and for life.

I want to suggest that the church at the level of the local parish must recover its role as the unifying institution of cultural life. It must again be the *cultus* in culture. In this activity not only is worship crucial but learning must be central. Christians are and have always been a people of the book. To establish the local parish as a center for learning would accomplish two things. First, it would contribute to the re-Christianization of culture by offering an alternative content to the tacit atheism of American public education. By transforming minds to think about knowledge and wisdom in categories of the Bible's metanarrative of creation, fall, and redemption, the parish school would offer a visionary and compelling "plausibility structure" for life and meaning to a generation hungering for certain and effectual knowledge. Second, the parish school offers parents a necessary vehicle for denying modernity. The parish school is a stopgap to a major conduit of modernity. In its smallness and locality it fosters community by bringing families together for the intentional cooperative effort of conserving and transmitting Christian culture. The parish school draws families, clergy, teachers, and others to the church more than once a week to accomplish the redeemed cultural task of education. In this mutual, covenantal activity, community is built in a very real, tangible, and essential way.

I am arguing, however, not just for parochialism but for catholic parochialism. To many this concept may sound like an oxymoron. What is universal localism? I would like to suggest that universal lo-

60. Niebuhr, *Christ and Culture*, 37.

calism or catholic parochialism is the scandal of the incarnation itself. You have heard it said, "Think globally and act locally." But I think the task of mission and ministry is to think locally and act globally. The end of our parochialism is not alien residency, but invasion. We are the church militant on the way to becoming the church triumphant — one holy catholic and apostolic church. We are God's salvation army of occupation in this world. The modest efforts at our parishes are to reorder our here and now cultural life in anticipation of the coming new world order. This is not a call to colonization but conquest.

My hope is to raise your vision for the biblical Christ in a pagan culture by lowering your sights to your particular parish context. Other ideas must be developed for the local parish to reach upward to God, inward to its member families, and outward to a lost and broken world. No grand plan, no universal strategic initiative, no telecommunications technology, no conference event, no definitive book, no comprehensive public policy has the potential to change hearts, minds, and lives in the profound way that you can by faithful ministry in your parish. We must demonstrate the reality of the incarnation in our words and walk at the parish level.

I am hopeful that a future book will be written centuries from now, if the Lord should tarry, entitled: *How the Anglicans Saved Civilization*.[61] The heroes of this book will be local parish priests and their families who understood the times with knowledge of what they should do.

61. I commend Thomas Cahill's excellent book entitled: *How the Irish Saved Civilization: The Untold Story of Ireland's Heroic Role from the Fall of Rome to the Rise of Medieval Europe* (New York: Doubleday, 1995), as a strategic model for continuing this discussion.

Christ and His Church:
The Implications of Christology
for the Mission of the Church Today

The Most Reverend & Right Honorable
GEORGE L. CAREY
Archbishop of Canterbury

The church, and the world, today are preparing for the end of the second Christian millennium. The end of an era is a good time to reflect on the past, examine the present, and make resolutions for the future; and our Anglican Communion must take full advantage of that. Most thoughtful people, of course, will be aware that the primary reason for this celebration is the impact that Jesus Christ has made on this world; an event which still empowers the church's mission and life.

This extraordinary figure of history still disturbs and still arouses controversy, both within the church and beyond. According to some Christians today, the time has come in these dying years of the twentieth century to make more modest claims for him. For others, the more obscure doctrines of the church hide the exciting person the millennium commemorates. For yet more people, a Christianity hidebound by rules and regulations has robbed the world and the church of the "real" Jesus. Such a contention is the argument, for instance, of a recent book, *Stealing Jesus,* by the American author, Bruce Bawer. By referring to the church as legalistic, Bawer is attacking fundamentalist versions of Christianity which see adherence to a selective set of doctrines and rules as the way to salvation. For Jesus, he argues, salvation wasn't a matter of pledging oneself to a set of commands; it was about universal compassion and love, unconditionally given. All the structures, doctrines, and interpretations of Scripture with which the church protects itself, for Bawer, falsify the attractive person at the center of the Christian faith.

The book ends with an illustration from Mark Twain's *Huckleberry Finn*. Having helped the slave Jim escape from his owner, Huck feels guilty about this deed, which others have told him is wrong and against the will of God. To avoid "everlasting fire," therefore, Huck writes to Miss Watson, Jim's owner, and tells her where Jim is hiding. He does so, and "feels good and all washed clean of sin for the first time I had ever felt so in my life." But then come second thoughts. Huck thinks of the fun they have and how sweet and good and gentle Jim is with him, and what a good friend he is. Holding the letter, Huck wrestles with his conscience. "I was trembling because I'd got to decide forever between two things and I knowed it. I studied a minute, sort of holding my breath, and then says to myself: 'All right then, I'll go to hell' — and tore it up." Bawer concludes: "And such is the kingdom of heaven."[1]

And many of us would agree — what Huckleberry did was right by the standards of humanity; and right, too, by the standards of Christ.

It is impossible to read the book unsympathetically. But as with so many popular distillations of doctrine, Bawer's book is broadly right in what it affirms, and wrong in what it denies. He is right to affirm the character of love as central to the Christian message, but he disregards the complexities of Christian ethics and history. His all too simplistic distinction between legalistic and nonlegalistic Christianity seems to lead to a rejection of law and doctrinal truth — and to the separation of Jesus Christ from apostolic teaching.

1. Bruce Bawer, *Stealing Jesus* (New York: Crown Publishing, 1997), 327.

I was moved to find in Bawer's book a generous tribute to the Anglican tradition: "Of all the major theological institutional approaches that grew out of the Protestant revolt, the Anglican theological method must surely commend itself to those who seek an intellectually solid, broadly inclusive foundation for a true church of love."[2] As President of the Anglican Communion it would be churlish of me to refute such a generous tribute; nor do I. I am glad that through this tradition Bawer found his way to baptism and into the body of Christ.

But it must be remembered, when the church is described affectionately as "broad," that it is not broad because it shares the romantic notions of a hostess who thinks that the best parties are ones where everyone disagrees. It is not broad because we don't really mind if people are Unitarians, or adoptionists, or atheists. The breadth exists because we share a common experience and belief, of God made manifest in Christ. We share a real understanding of Christ as God incarnate. The experience has come in many ways: through the Bible, through the sacraments, through Christian witness, through prayer, even through an actual confrontation with Christ. It may well be the case that it is our experience which is diverse, but that experience leads us towards a common faith in Christ; this experience of Christ is the "wideness" in God's mercy, and we are drawn into the body of Christ, the church, which provides us with a framework within which our disparate journeys can draw closer together.

At the heart of the church will always be this living Christ, and our experience of him is the guide for our mission. This search for definition and clarity, for cutting one face from the collage and claiming that it is the whole picture, must end here in the mission of the church. For in the context of Christlike mission, the doctrine preached will not be fossilized and cold; and neither will our Jesus be simply the easy humanist beloved by so many seekers after the "real" Jesus. The true Jesus who is exposed in the Gospels is a far more complex character. His cryptic sayings, his elusive parables, his mysterious silences, his commanding presence — this extraordinary

2. Bawer, *Stealing Jesus,* 64.

ministry was punctuated with a language of violence against the callousness of the conventional world. He said difficult things — that he came as a "sword" to divide brother from brother, to turn wife against husband and family against himself. Difficult things, indeed — but those first Christians knew what he meant. And if *our* mission is Christlike, no one will doubt what we are saying or doing. So, our understanding of Jesus is central to the mission of the church. Indeed, it turns out to be the very foundation stone of ecclesiology — the stone on which we build — or, conversely, the "stone that causes men to stumble." There are no half measures here. He is the only justification for the existence of the church and, as we approach the next millennium, he will be what he has always been — the heart of its life and future.

Yes, we claim, however embarrassing it may seem these days, that the climax of human history came in the form of a humble carpenter's son from a minor province of the Roman Empire in the first century AD. We certainly experience, from time to time, the icy blasts of scorn and contempt for such an intellectual commitment to a person who lived so long ago and in such unfamiliar circumstances. While theology must engage constantly with serious scholarship and criticism, we should recall that St. Paul tells us that three things abide, and one of them was not intellectual erudition or passing intellectual fashion. They were love, hope, and *faith*. If Jesus Christ is the heart of the church's life, then he is her glory and pride. One implication of that is that if the church today does not live and work that out in faith and hope and love, the battle is lost and the millennium is for us all a rather pointless and fruitless celebration.

Let me offer you two examples from the lives of two former Archbishops — perhaps two of the best known. Fourteen hundred years ago, Augustine set out nervously with forty equally fearful monks from Rome for England. He had not gone very far when murmurings amongst his team, and his own fears of that hostile and savage country "Britain," overwhelmed him, and the party turned back to Rome. But Gregory the Great would not sympathize with Augustine's fears. He reminded them that they were called to a life of prayer; and that they must have faith in the passionate commitment they shared — to witness to the claims of Christ. If they were loyal to the Jesus they knew, they need not fear the "barbarous, fierce, and pagan" warriors of Britain. Gregory wrote to the party, saying, as Bede records:

> "My very dear sons, it is better never to undertake any high enterprise than to abandon it when once begun . . . with the help of God you must carry out this holy task which you have begun. Be constant and zealous in carrying out this enterprise which, under God's guidance, you have undertaken."[3]

Augustine was inspired anew and returned to his mission, determined to succeed. And, let us be clear, he sailed from France with a *church*, indeed a Christ-centered church. Yet this does not mean that he crossed the channel accompanied by the House of Bishops, guided by the General Synod or the General Convention, in a boat supplied and rowed by the Church Commissioners! He came with a faithful community of monks who were devoted to embodying the living Christ in mission. This was what sustained the first Archbishop of Canterbury. The replanting of the church in southern England, starting in Canterbury, owes a great deal to the simplicity of discipleship lived by ordinary people in the power of the Holy Spirit. It was still a very human church, however, full of devotion and love, and it could not utterly attain the goal it set itself. We remember Augustine's later arrogance and discourtesy in assuming that the Celtic bishops he met at Aust (near our present-day Bristol) were an inferior episcopacy. These marks of weakness showed again at the Synod of Whitby, when the Celtic tradition, the older form of faith in the North, was displaced by a triumphalist Roman model. Alas, so often the story of faithful, sacrificial mission and ministry is also the story of our failure to live up to the nature of our calling. So when we speak of a Christ-centered church, we speak not of something which is pure and perfect, but of people, seeking to live together in faith, hope, and love, always alert to the transforming Spirit of God who will lead them into all truth.

We turn now from the first to the hundredth Archbishop,

---

3. Bede, *A History of the English Church and People* (Harmondsworth: Penguin, 1955), 67.

much-loved Michael Ramsey. For him, everything good and interesting about the church was christological. Following Christ implied a devotion to holiness; and the church was the new Israel, a people chosen to be holy in each and every generation. But his generation was living in the 1960s, and everything, including the church, was either being discovered anew, or rejected altogether. No less than John Robinson, with whom, following *Honest to God*, he had many fascinating theological encounters, Ramsey was passionately committed to the renewal of the church. But his was a different approach. Robinson, as we know, saw the process as inevitably involving the deconstruction of theology and structures. Reform meant to "re-form" every aspect of faith and life; of the words and pictures we use to talk about God, and of the church itself. Ramsey was convinced otherwise. His underlying conviction was that Christ was enough. A wholehearted affirmation of his life, death, and resurrection, and a call to prayer and holiness of life, was as effective now as ever. He did not disagree with Robinson that Christian faith had to be brought into line with modern culture. Simply, as Rowan Williams[4] has pointed out, he did not see any tension between that culture and Christian belief. God was still God and the relevance of the Christian faith was immediately available to those prepared to commit themselves to the living God. Once again, the right message, the successful message was — don't be afraid and don't be ashamed to confess the faith of Christ crucified. It is interesting, by the way, to read *Robinson's* Christology nearly forty years on. By the standards of some theologians today, it is solid, traditional, incarnational. In fact, rather similar in many respects to that of Michael Ramsey.

This absolute faith in Christ, and in the power and relevance of Christ, is central to the church for two reasons. Firstly, it is both the essence and substance of the church, its reason to be and its being. Secondly, it shows the way in which it is effective, for the effectiveness of the church depends on the extent to which it communicates the divine to the human: and in Jesus, we believe that these two realms found perfect communion.

4. In Robin Gill and Lorna Kendall, eds., *Michael Ramsey as Theologian* (Boston: Cowley, 1995).

This first point that faith in Christ is the essence and substance of the church challenges privatized forms of Christianity. We
all know of people whose dislike of the conventional church leads to
a rejection of institutional Christianity. Bewildered by the doctrinal
difficulties of our day, exasperated by the complex web of church
structures, fed up by dissent between the different church bodies,
some retire into a private world of faith. I understand their frustra-
tions, but abandoning the church won't help them. John Henry
Newman made a robust criticism of this attitude 165 years ago
when he said:

> Almighty God might have left Christianity as a sort of sacred liter-
> ature, as contained in the Bible, which every person was to take
> and use by himself. . . . This, I say, he might have done but he has
> ordained otherwise. He has actually set up a society, which exists
> even to this day all over the world, and which (as a general rule)
> Christians are bound to join so that to believe in Christ is not a
> mere opinion or a secret conviction, but a social and even political
> principle.[5]

Divorced from the common tradition and the testing of private opinion against the faith of others, manipulation of truth becomes all too easy for self-centered human beings.

So if we are bound to join the church, if the fact of Christ is indeed comprehensive, inviting corporate and even universal action,
then the church is bound in turn to live by its missionary obligations, for mission is at the heart of the challenge of the gospel. The
cross of Jesus Christ is not a question mark to puzzle over, but a
thrilling adventure for all to take up gladly and devotedly. Jesus
Christ is the reason for the church: and respond to Jesus Christ is
what the church does. Given that this response is necessarily evangelistic, mission is not, then, an optional extra for the church, but one
of its most important defining marks.

Thus Jürgen Moltmann in his *Jesus Christ for Today's World*
draws attention to the secondary nature of the church after Christ
himself. Earlier in this work, he describes Jesus as "the kingdom of

---

5. J. H. Newman, *Tracts for the Times* No. 2: "The Catholic Church" (1833).

God in person." Now for the church to discover Jesus again in the modern world, it must, in a telling phrase, "make the kingdom of God the church's lodestone."[6] The kingdom of God, the dynamic human and divine Christ, must be the magnetic core of the church: the lodestone that guides it, that gives it weight and balance, and that draws people towards it. Without this christological center, says Moltmann, the church is not really a church at all.

And this brings me on to my second point. For if the church is to be effective in its mission, it must express, as far as it can, the communion between the human and the divine which is Jesus Christ. For the kingdom of God to be the church's lodestone we must undertake the task of what Moltmann calls "evangelization and liberation." That is not only bringing people to Christ, but also making a Christlike people. These two activities complement each other — "like the raising up through faith of the soul that is bowed down and the healing of the tormented body."[7] This was realized clearly in the recent Lambeth Conference, where the dedication to ecumenism, the clarity of doctrine, and the importance of our unity as a Communion (all evangelization issues) were discussed alongside the liberation issues of Third World debt and human rights. The apostolic witness and ministry demands that we are involved in Christianizing every possible area of human life. In baptism, we say "I turn to Christ." That is the whole person in every context and in all relationships, so part of our mission is to seek constantly to conform to that promise.

This ministry was described best in the Pauline concept of the church as the body of Christ, the visible body of Christ in the world. Now, there are not too many people who would argue with that as a model for the church. But it presents a problem that the church has never solved. For the church as the embodiment of Christ must signify, as I said earlier, the human and the divine. It must demonstrate the human Jesus striving for holiness and liberation in the Israel of his day, and ultimately suffering for it; and it must also demonstrate the power and faithfulness of God, displayed for all time in the res-

6. Jürgen Moltmann, *Jesus Christ for Today's World* (London: SCM, 1994), 7, 27.
7. Moltmann, *Jesus Christ for Today's World,* 28.

urrection. And so a missionary ecclesiology founded on the incarnate Christ creates inescapable tensions, a few of which I propose to discuss here. We must work on the clashes between service and status, between holiness and legalism, and spirit and structures.

Service and Status

Archbishops are, more than most, uncomfortably aware of the tension between service and status. I was told at my enthronement as Bishop of Bath and Wells: "From now on you will experience two things; you will never lack for a good meal, but also, from now on no one will ever tell you the truth." I admit the first is usually true, but I trust people *will* tell me the truth if I am prepared to listen carefully, and to listen to uncomfortable things. However, those of us in leadership must acknowledge that, sometimes, the trappings of leadership get in the way of the listening that makes for effective leadership. While it is clear that in any organization there must be leaders who speak, decide, and act on behalf of others, too often status, honor, rank, and privilege have created barriers around those in authority, and especially between clergy and laity. It is a sign of our failure in this regard that the phrase "going into the church" as a euphemism for ordination remains common parlance.

The incarnation reminds us that there can be no real ministry without that emptying of self (kenosis) implied in common and humble service and grateful surrender to our Lord. The radical simplicity of obedience is a missing element in much of modern Christian ministry because we are so brainwashed by a world which assumes that self-advancement, self-fulfillment, and self-gratification are the ways in which we advance as human beings, even as Christian human beings. The most powerful and evocative symbols of a true church are still lives surrendered in ministry to our Lord.

Take, for instance, St. Francis, who, despite his absolute obedience to his ecclesiastical masters, was never ordained priest, preferring to set up a Christlike mission in weakness and confraternity, going forward into the world to serve, giving fresh inspiration to the office of deacon. Or look at that great lover of the very poor and unloved, Mother Teresa, who inspired so many in an apparently secular world. It is at once surprising and unsurprising that these lives should be so effective. Surprising, because it runs counter to contemporary expectations whether of ourselves or others; and unsurprising too, because such virtues as integrity, holiness, and sacrifice lie deep within the human condition, however hard-nosed and cynical we may be. This is vital for Christology. For as Gerry O'Collins says in *Interpreting Jesus:* "To improve Christology, we need better scholarship and better discipleship."[8]

This is the way that the church is effective — not just through clearer doctrine but through clearer discipleship. Recently I asked the head of a large school, where many outsiders came to take assemblies, who, in his opinion, were the most popular speakers with the teenagers. He replied without hesitation: "Members of religious communities." Young people, in other words, recognize and understand radical commitment and are moved and challenged by simple obedience.

But we must not think that only well-publicized and outreaching religious communities can serve effectively in this way. To speak of the church in sacramental terms, which I believe to be legitimate, is to speak of the presence of Christ through the daily witness of worship, service, and daily living of every Christian. There are many places in our world today where Christians cannot engage in overt mission and evangelism. To do so is to court persecution. In such cases, "being there" as signs of grace is the only option. But it is an option that God continues to use to his glory. The recent Lambeth Conference gave many graphic illustrations of this. That bishop in an Islamic country, unable to wear a dog collar and a pectoral cross — forbidden symbols — whose ministry of invisible care and nurture among Christians of all denominations continues, by God's grace, to bequeath new Christians. Or an African bishop and his wife who seek out their scattered flock behind the battle lines, sharing their poverty and bringing God's hope and love amidst such awful suffering. That Western bishop whose own experience of intense personal

8. Gerald O'Collins, *Interpreting Jesus* (London: Geoffrey Chapman/Mowbray, 1983), 207.

suffering has led her to be able to identify so much more vividly with the suffering of others. Those many — too many — African bishops and clergy who continue their faithful ministries in spite of erratic payment of salaries. All these are examples that give hope and focus to what it is to be a leader in God's church. They have reconciled the tension between service and status, whereby their status informs their service, and their service informs their status. Their lives speak so powerfully of the reconciliation of human and divine in the body of Christ.

And just as Christ's reconciliation of heaven with earth was sealed in his death, so death is the seal of these Christlike missions. "When Christ calls a man," declared Bonhoeffer long ago, "he bids him come and die." Death continues to be a sign of apostolic ministry; death to personal ambition, death to self-gratification, death to the pomp and status that cloak poverty of spirituality. In my Presidential Address at the Thirteenth Lambeth Conference I called for a renewal of our life as bishops, for a ministry of service, following the pattern laid down by our Lord in washing his disciples' feet. I said:

> At times, we can be tempted by an office dignified by the trappings of robes and ornate pageantry. Some have further identified episcopacy with a lofty style of autocratic leadership. We must never avoid the real challenges of Episcopal leadership. For that challenge is to follow our Lord in such simplicity of discipleship that our goodness, our holiness, our humility is there for all to see.

There is, I went on to say, a true glory in such leadership — and I have seen it again and again as I have traveled the Anglican Communion. Humble, sacrificial, devoted service continues, and is central to the renewal of the church.

Holiness and Legalism

I began this chapter by referring to Bawer's attack on what he called "legalistic Christianity." We live at a time when many argue that they wish to be free from the restrictions of law which seem to impede human freedom and fulfillment.

Perhaps law and legalism in Christianity today do seem far from the heart, from our innermost selves, and from the heart of true holiness. We know the history of the church: we can see clearly the tendency to codify the obligations of discipleship in rigid law. We can see how this can fossilize the freshness and compelling quality of simple obedience: a process analogous for some to the obscuration of the simple and compassionate Jesus of history by the church's creature, Christ as liberator of hell and potentate of time — a contrast which I have already rejected.

Edward Schillebeeckx complains of this "rigidification" in his *The Church with a Human Face*. For him, the Gospel of Love was all too quickly replaced by a "theological legitimization of relationships of subjection and power which are essentially contrary to the gospel." He is not challenging holiness or law. Rather, he is correctly pointing out that the Christian faith expects holiness to proceed from baptism and challenges all our attempts to codify it. In a telling criticism of forms of priesthood which rely on constructs of theological justification, he comments: "Many priests who are dedicated to a believing community and are not burdened with a 'doctrine of the priestly character' thus show that in practice they have a deeper understanding of what the traditional faith understands by 'character' than others who defend verbally the 'ontological character,' and do not know what it really comprises." As for so many Christians, for Schillebeeckx, "the failure with the Church legalism is its failure to see the depths of the mystery."[9] Instead of fathoming something infinitely profound at the root of our being, the church so often jumps at ideologies instead.

But just as the possible conflict between a Jesus of history and a Christ of tradition can be resolved by seeking to encounter Christ, wherever we may find him, so also this conflict between holiness undefined, and legalism defined, must be resolved in Christ. It is in the living out of a Christian faith that a truly Christlike ministry for the church is discovered.

9. Edward Schillebeeckx, *The Church with a Human Face* (London: SCM, 1985), 69.

The question is important because it has implications for our mission. For a mission will not be effective if a church is divided against itself. Again, this has been made clear to me by the experience of the Lambeth Conference. Two issues were discussed about which the church seems uncertain — human sexuality, and the relationship between Christianity and other faiths. On sexuality, there were calls from some people whose view of holiness seemed to suggest a codification of sexual practices to regulate Christian behavior; on the other hand there were some whose view of holiness seemed to allow a total openness and unconditional acceptance of all patterns of behavior. Similarly with the interaction between Christianity and other world faiths, there were those who wanted clear boundaries to be drawn, whilst others were content with blurred edges and to live with the questions. In both cases, two apparently distinct worlds of holiness and legalistic authority seemed to be in conflict with one another.

Of course, only God can fully integrate both. But we are a human church and we must seek a balance between them. In both cases, I think, we were successful, giving firm moral leadership on sexuality whilst upholding that compassion which is the primary duty of the church; and commending greater understanding between Christianity and other faiths, whilst maintaining our commitment to the finality of Christian revelation.

You see, the holiness which we seek is neither a holiness simply drawn from written law nor from the permissiveness of our culture. We are called to a radical obedience to Jesus Christ who invites us deeper into his crucified and risen life and faithfulness. Indeed, to return to the Lambeth Resolutions, in order for our mission to thrive, we must strive to achieve the sort of church which emerges from those resolutions — a church which is open to all people, which suffers, in the most literal sense of the word, all things; and which is yet utterly secure in its own identity and calling to be the body of Christ in the world. Our openness should not become a cynical license of everything in our society; our security must not become a severe legalism where the compassion of Christ is whittled away by rigid delineation.

William Temple, it is said, once stated: "I believe in One Holy,

Catholic, and Apostolic Church — but regret that it doesn't exist."
In *Christus Veritas,* he made a similar point:

> The Ideal Church does not exist and has never existed; some day,
> here or elsewhere it will exist, meanwhile its members are also
> members of "the world" . . . for this reason, we ought not in strict-
> ness ever to speak of the failure of the Church; we should speak of
> the failure of Christians. The failure that is conspicuous enough
> in history, is a failure of Christian people to be thoroughly Chris-
> tian. The true Church does not fail; but the true Church is still
> coming slowly into existence; that process is the meaning of His-
> tory from the Incarnation onwards.[10]

Recognition of our failure is the precondition of our future
unity as the church. It is the recognition that holiness and legalism
are not separate in our Savior: and our mission to the world is not to
preach the perfect church, which is yet to be, but the Lord who is the
heart of its worship and life.

Spirit and Structure

Besides law as a precondition for government, there is also the question of structures. Often it is the structures of the church that are
resented so bitterly by its critics. So much of the bureaucracy can
seem utterly removed from what is loosely termed the spirit of
Christianity. But it would be wrong to see the spirit of Christianity
as being a sort of simplistic mysticism. I have already spoken of the
danger of seeing the corporate element of Christianity as being an
optional extra. It must be recognized that structures are essential
for that corporate life.

Even that most mystical of theologians, Hans Urs von Balthasar,
saw that mysticism was only the obverse of hierarchy, the spirit the
obverse of structure. He also saw that both must be combined in the
service of the whole church's even deeper appropriation and understanding of life in Christ. Experience of God for von Balthasar is not

10. William Temple, *Christus Veritas* (London: Macmillan, 1925), 238.

enough: there has to be obedience to God following from that. This obedience is to the knowledge of God seen in company with other members of the faithful. Mark McIntosh has said in a study of von Balthasar's thought: "Authentic Christian spirituality is already communally oriented, for it is a spirituality ordered primarily to obedience, which always involves community." Von Balthasar not only understood this truth. He tried to embody it in his secular institute, the Community of St. John, which attempted to combine the church of love (Mary) with the church of hierarchy (St. Peter). Here there were two characteristic notes: "obedience to Christ," and "the ability to disappear into the Church." Structures in the church only become stumbling blocks if we allow ourselves to use them for personal power, and self-projection. Anonymity within the church is what makes the spirit (or Spirit) of Christianity visible. McIntosh concludes: "The central criterion of authentic spirituality would be a sharing in Christ's total availability to serve God's work in the world, a sharing that is in no way self-seeking, or even self-conscious."[11]

We don't have to be Roman Catholics to echo that theology. I regret that sometimes I meet Anglicans whose criticism of their own church indicates that they do not love it and are not committed to it. And such attitudes separate Christology and ecclesiology, for Ephesians tells us that: "Christ loved the church and gave himself for her."

Yes, the self-denial of which McIntosh speaks has to be undertaken on a christological basis. Just as we emulate the self-emptying of Christ in our service to the world, we do so in commitment and love to his church.

We turn to Moltmann again, whose concept of the Open Church has been such an influence on my own thinking. His words are disturbing but liberating: "The Church is not there for its own sake. It is there for the sake of Jesus' concern. All the Church's own interests — its continuation in its existing form, the extension of its influence — must be subordinated to the interests of the Kingdom of God, and help us to know Christ."

11. Mark McIntosh, *Christology from Within: Spirituality and Incarnation in Hans Urs von Balthasar* (Notre Dame: University of Notre Dame Press, 1996), 19-20.

Perhaps as a clue as to how we may bring spirit and structure together in order to make Christ known, we should look at worship as an analogy to the practical machinery of the church. The liturgy, the outward act, is equivalent to our structures. The inward act of worship or communion is equivalent to the spirit. Now, we all know of services where the aesthetics are sublime, and the formalities are performed with militaristic precision: and the whole is perfect to an almost narcissistic extent. Similarly, we have been to services where many people are saying in a great cacophonous testimony what Christ has done for them and where the worship is powerfully challenging and disturbing.

In both cases, we might suspect, the outsider, the newcomer, the visitor, the *non-Christian,* might be sitting in the midst of either, trying to find a point at which they feel at home. But those are the extremes. Far more common, I believe, is the experience, in many parts of the Anglican Communion, in churches evangelical or catholic in their tradition, of the liturgy feeding the worship and serving it unobtrusively, while at the same time making it accessible to everybody.

Now if this is a common experience in worship, we need to ask why can't it be a common experience at every level of church life? Structure serving spirit, and spirit made comprehensible by structure. An engagement, we might say, between the human and divine.

It is obvious from this analogy, I hope, that the most important implication of Christology for the church today is that we become most Christlike when at the center of all our activities are the great facts of the cross and resurrection. Indeed, without the passion and the risen life of the human and divine Christ, the human and divine church cannot become the body of Christ. Rowan Williams states how the living Christ transforms all human categories:

The resurrection of Jesus makes it impossible to take for granted that the world is nothing but a system of oppressors and victims, an endless cycle of reactive violence. We are free to understand ourselves and each other in a new way, as living in mutual gift not mutual threat. We can collaborate in the relations that the resurrection sets in motion, relations of forgiveness, equality and care when we "know Jesus."[12]

The survival of the church, therefore, does not depend upon its structures alone, or on its structure-less outpourings of Spirit. It depends on how far we can make the synods, councils, and machinery of the church a promised community of mutual gift, not mutual threat. It depends on how far we are able as the body of Christ, to give of ourselves completely freely, in service to the world, in holiness to God, and in commitment to the Christlike mission of the church.

In the perception of the world there are so many models of the church. The church as bureaucracy, the church as institutionalized morality, the church as social service, the church as the school of liberal humanism, the church as the holy arm of the body politic, the church as obedient yet troubled wife of the secular state. These impressions must be challenged and changed. They must be replaced with a model of the church as the sacrament of Christ, of his incarnate nature, and of his act of gratuitous love for the world in his cross and resurrection. The church can only become this sacramental sign if it gives itself unreservedly to living and proclaiming Christ as Lord and Hope of Glory — the Christ of whom Pascal once said "is a God whom we can approach without pride and before whom we can humble ourselves without despair." Yes, the implications are costly and disturbing, but if we take this Christ deeply into our life, deeply into our structures and laws, deeply into our synods and debates, we shall walk confidently into the new millennium with a gospel worth proclaiming. It will be the gospel of the Christlike church; a church worth belonging to — because it truly, and authentically, belongs to him.

12. Rowan Williams, "Foreword" to *Knowing Jesus* by James Alison (London: SPCK, 1993).

Contributors

The Most Rev. and Rt. Hon. George L. Carey, Archbishop of Canterbury

The Rev. Dr. Christopher D. Hancock, Vicar, Holy Trinity, Cambridge; former Professor of Theology, Virginia Theological Seminary

The Rev. Dr. Richard Reid, former Dean and Professor of New Testament Studies, Virginia Theological Seminary

The Rev. Dr. N. T. Wright, Dean, Lichfield Cathedral, author

The Rev. Dr. Alister McGrath, Principle, Wycliffe Hall, Oxford, author

Alan R. Crippen II, Senior Fellow for religion and political studies at The Witherspoon Fellowship, Washington, D.C.